CREWE TO MANCHESTER

Vic Mitchell and Keith Smith

MP Middleton Press

Front cover: Red livery had been prevalent on the route for coaching stock since 1923, but blue locomotives were still a recent idea when no. E3001 was photographed at Crewe with a Manchester to Euston train on 3rd September 1967. Blue was sometimes tried on express locomotives after nationalisation. (M.J.Stretton)

Back cover upper: Stockport is being approached by no. 47341 on 12th June 1961. It is hauling a Merry-Go-Round train, so called as it never reversed at colliery or power station. (P.Jones)

Back cover lower: Many new colour combinations were steadily evolved. This is EMU no. 303048 at Manchester Piccadilly on 14th March 1989. Few would have then thought that trams would eventually be running under their feet here. (M.J.Stretton)

Published April 2014

ISBN 978 1 908174 57 4

© Middleton Press, 2014

Design Deborah Esher
Typesetting Barbara Mitchell

Published by
    Middleton Press
    Easebourne Lane
    Midhurst
    West Sussex
    GU29 9AZ
Tel: 01730 813169
Fax: 01730 812601
Email: info@middletonpress.co.uk
www.middletonpress.co.uk

Printed in the United Kingdom by Henry Ling Limited, at the Dorset Press, Dorchester, DT1 1HD

INDEX

32	Alderley Edge	61	Handforth	109	Manchester London Road
57	Burnage	48	Heald Green	114	Manchester Piccadilly
64	Cheadle Hulme	96	Heaton Chapel	59	Mauldeth Road
28	Chelford	89	Heaton Norris	19	Middlewich
1	Crewe	23	Holmes Chapel	10	Sandbach
55	East Didsbury	101	Levenshulme	78	Stockport
52	Gatley	104	Longsight	43	Styal
26	Goostrey	45	Manchester Airport	38	Wilmslow

Northwich Branch 15-22
Styal Line 43-60

ACKNOWLEDGEMENTS

We are very grateful for the assistance received from many of those mentioned in the credits, also to A.R.Carder, A.J.Castledine, G.Croughton, G.Gartside, D.A.Johnson, N.Langridge, B.Lewis, J.P.McCrickard, Mr. D. and Dr S.Salter, T.Walsh and in particular, our always supportive wives, Barbara Mitchell and Janet Smith.

I. The diagrams are from the 1964 LMR timetable and this one shows the entire route. Map II has the details of the lines north of Alderley Edge at a larger scale. The line from Sandbach to Northwich via Middlewich is not shown as it closed to passengers on 4th January 1960.

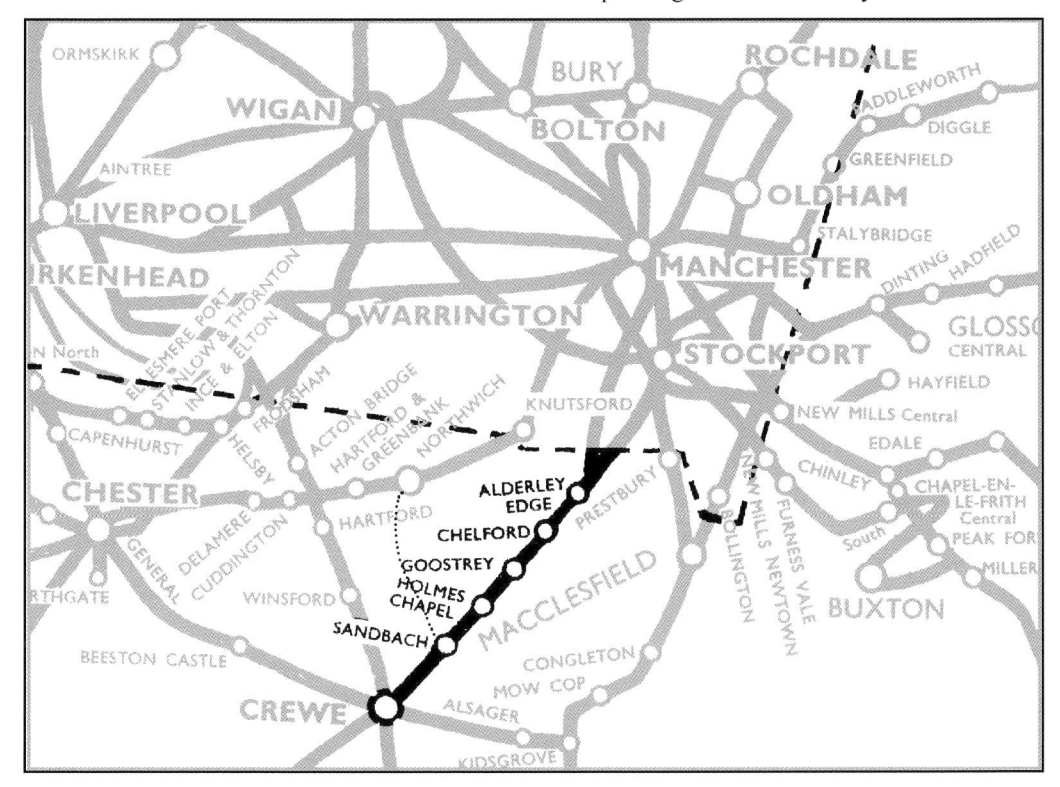

GEOGRAPHICAL SETTING

     Crewe was a tiny community prior to the arrival of the railway. Dwellings of dull red brick proliferated as the famous works grew, following the arrival of six routes. The journey illustrated in this album is across the eastern part of the Cheshire Plain, which is based on red sandstones.

     While the western part is drained by the River Dee, the area over which we will travel has watercourses running into the River Dane at Middlewich and subsequently the River Weaver at Northwich. The tributaries of the Mersey which meander across the Cheshire Plain were crossed by several viaducts - Ladybrook (near Cheadle), the Dean (near Handforth), the Bollin (near Wilmslow), the Peover (near Chelford), the Dane (near Holmes Chapel) and the Wheelock (near Sandbach).

     At Stockport there is a spectacular crossing of the River Mersey at a great height. A steady descent to Manchester follows. The city is famed for the manufacture of cotton goods, benefitting a population of over 50,000 before the coming of the railways.

     The main minerals worked in the area were salt and gravel, the former resulting in much land settlement, notably around Middlewich.

     The southern section of the route was built in Cheshire and the northern part in Lancashire. The maps are to the scale of 25ins to 1 mile, with north at the top, unless otherwise indicated.

II.   This diagram continues from Alderley Edge to Wilmslow, which is shown at the bottom of this 1964 extract. The Styal Line branches left there and bypasses Stockport.

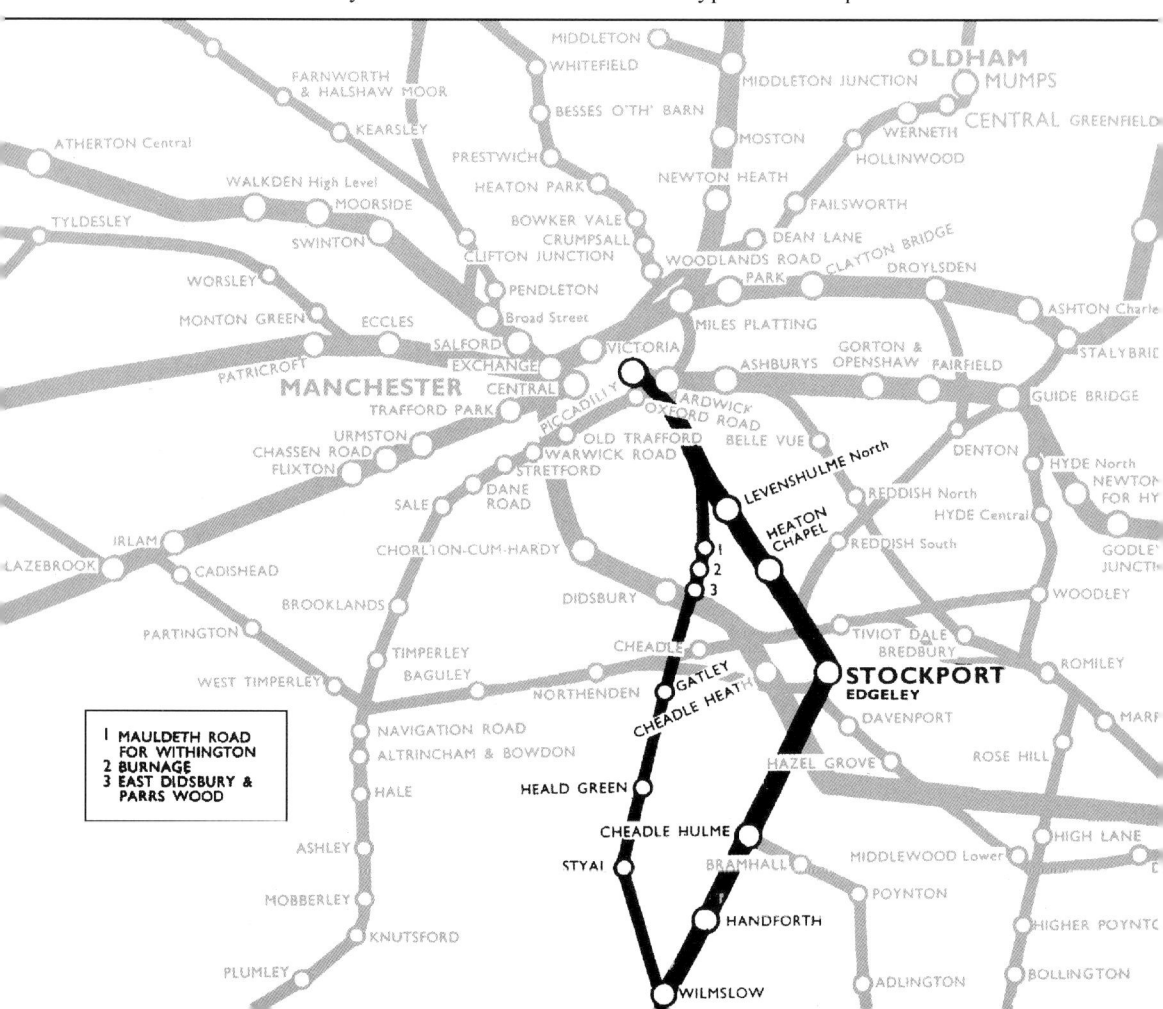

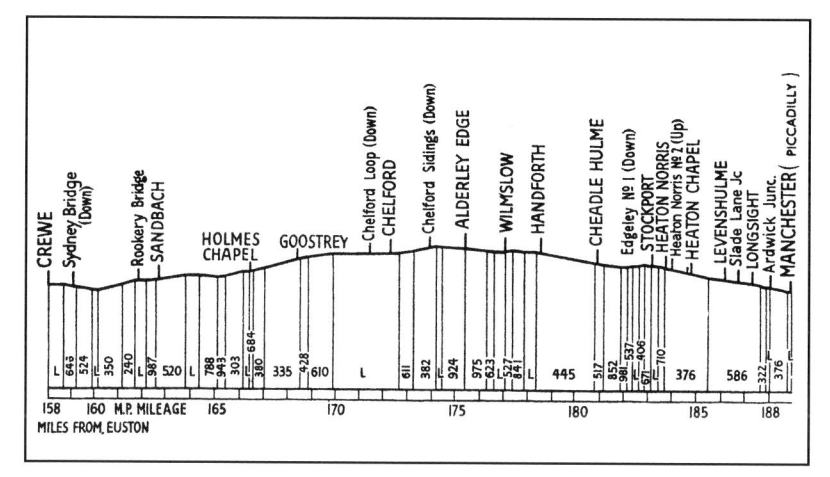

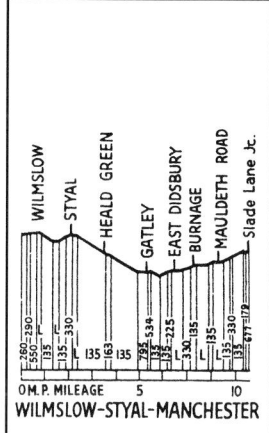

Gradient profiles

HISTORICAL BACKGROUND

The first line in the area was that of the Liverpool & Manchester Railway, this opening in 1830. The London & Birmingham Railway was completed in 1838. The Grand Junction Railway was finished in 1837 and linked the other two railways, via Crewe and Warrington.

The Manchester & Birmingham Railway received its Act in 1837 and it opened between Manchester (Travis Street) and Stockport (Heaton Norris) on 4th June 1840. It was extended to London Road in Manchester and to Crewe on 10th May 1842. All these companies became part of the London & North Western Railway in 1846. Manchester also received trains from Bolton in 1838, from Leeds in 1839, from Sheffield in 1842, from Altrincham in 1849, Huddersfield also 1849 and from Marple in 1862. (See map XXIII, near picture 77 for details).

Crewe had links from Chester in 1840, from Kidsgrove in 1848 and from Nantwich in 1858. The route from Kidsgrove to Sandbach opened for goods in 1852. It ran through Middlewich to Northwich from 1867, carrying passengers from 1st July 1868 to 4th January 1960. The loop through Styal was built under an Act of 1899 and opened on 1st May 1909.

The LNWR became part of the London Midland & Scottish Railway in 1923. This largely became the London Midland Region of British Railways upon nationalisation in 1948.

Electric services started in the area on the Styal Line on 21st January 1959. They began on the West Coast Main Line from Crewe to Manchester on 12th September 1960 and between Crewe and Liverpool on 1st January 1962. The new standard of 25kV at 50 cycles was used. Stafford to Crewe electric services began on 7th January 1963 and they reached London on 6th November 1965.

The branch to Manchester Airport received trains from 17th May 1993, but the southern spur of the junction did not open until 15th January 1996.

Following the Railways Act of November 1993, privatisation resulted in five operating companies usually providing the service. Most began in 1997, but the franchise durations varied. They included North Western Trains, Regional Railways North East (south to Manchester Airport), CrossCountry, Virgin West Coast Trains and Wales & West. Ten years later, the list showed Northern Rail, TransPennine Express, CrossCountry and Virgin Trains.

PASSENGER SERVICES

The weekday down frequency is shown, with Sunday figures in brackets. The first 5¼ miles opened with 13(4) in 1840, this rising in 1842 to 19(4) starting at Stockport, plus 7(4) from Crewe. By 1850, these figures were 18(8) and 9(5).

The local service increased steadily and so just the Crewe - Manchester trains will be listed hereon. Short journeys are excluded.

	Non-stop to Stockport		Semi-fast		Most stations	
	Weekdays	Sundays	Weekdays	Sundays	Weekdays	Sundays
1880	5	3	7	1	8	2
1910	10	4	3	2	10	3
1940	7	9	5	2	9	2

From around 1960, regular interval services had been worked by local trains.

Styal Line

From 1909 to 1939 down trains on weekdays ran every 15 minutes until noon, every 30 minutes thereafter and at peak times at 15 minute intervals. On Sundays there were less.

Dieselisation in 1956 and subsequent electrification brought regular "clock face" timetables.

April 1880

July 1910

CREWE, ALDERLEY EDGE, GATLEY, STOCKPORT, and MANCHESTER.—L. & N. W.

District Pass. Supt., S. B. Carter, Exchange Station, Manchester. District Goods Man., W. J. Chipman, Manchester.

Miles from Crewe.	Miles from Crewe.	Down.	Week Days.																		
		Euston Station,	aft	ngt.	ngt.	mrn	mrn	mrn	mrn	mrn	mrn	mrn	mrn	mrn	mrn	mrn	mrn	mrn	mrn	mrn	mrn
				Sleeping Saloon, London to Manchester. Except Mondays.	Sleeping Saloon, London to Manchester. Mondays only.											Except Saturdays. Birmingham Express.			Via Macclesfield.		Breakfast Cars, London to Crewe.
		404London ....dep.	10 0	12 0	12 0									5 0					7 10	7 10	8 30
		404Birmingham † ... "	11o0	2 50	3 10							6 0		7 20		8 30		9 10	9 15	9 15	9 55
		458Bristol (Tem. Md.) "		1225t																	
		458Shrewsbury .... "	mrn	3t40										6 55				8 55		10 0	
—	—	Crewe ....dep.	2 0	4 35	5 0		6 40		7 25			8 5		9 8		9 46	9 50	1035		1115	1148
4⅝	4⅝	Sandbach	2 8				6 53		7 35			8 20	8 50	9 16			9 58			1125	
8⅝	8⅝	Holmes Chapel					7 1		7 42			8 28	8 57				1010			1133	
10⅝	10⅝	Goostrey					7 8		7 47			8 33	9 2				1014				
14¼	14¼	Chelford, for Knutsford..	2 23				7 19		7 55			8 42	9 11				1022			1144	
17¼	17¼	Alderley Edge		c	c	7 5	7 29		8 4	8 15	8 35	8 51	9 19		9 45		1033	1056	k	1151	
18⅞	18⅞	Wilmslow				7 8	7 35	8 0	8 10	8 20	8 39	8 57	9 25		9 49		1038			1156	
—	20⅜	Styal						8 4			8 44				9 54						
—	22⅛	Heald Green						8 8			8 48				9 58						
—	23¾	Gatley ....[Wood						8 12			8 52				10 2						
—	25	East Didsbury & Parr's						8 15			8 56				10 5						
—	—	Burnage						8 18							10 8						
—	26⅝	Mauldeth Road *						8 21			9 0				1011						
20¼	—	Handforth				7 12	7 40		8 15	8 25		9 2	9 29				1043			12 1	
22⅛	—	Cheadle Hulme 529 [526				7 17	7 47		8 21	8 31							1049				
25	—	Stockport ¶ 503, 520, arr	2 42	5 10	5 35	7 24	7 54			8 37		9 14	9 39	9 45			1055	11 9	1155	12 9	1218
30¾	30⅝	Manchester ¶ 503, 505 London Rd. "	3 0	5 26	5 50	7 37	8 8	8c30	8 42	8 55	9c10	9 28	9 52	10 0	1020	1030	1110	1122	1210	1222	1230
31½	31⅛	Oxford Rd. "																			
36½	—	Victoria .. "																			

Down.	Week Days—*Continued.*																					
Euston Station,	aft	mrn	mrn	aft	aft	mrn		mrn	aft	mrn	aft	aft	aft	aft	aft	aft	aft	aft	aft	aft	aft	aft
						Luncheon Car Express.	To Colne, see pp. 766 & 744.					Luncheon Car Express.			Via Macclesfield.				London, Dover, Bournemouth, Eastbourne, and Brighton Express, see page 406.			
404London ....dep.						1030				u1037		1210			1215		1225	1 30	2 40			
404Birmingham † ... "			1115							1210				2 20				3 30				
458Bristol (Tem. Md.) "			9t0					9t30									t1245					
458Shrewsbury .... "			1155					1238						2 18			3t40					
Crewe ....dep.		1210	1248		1 10			1 42		2 15		3 10		3 49		4 0	4 34	5 10	5 38			5 55
Sandbach		1220								2 24						4 10						6 5
Holmes Chapel		1228								M.S						4 18						6 13
Goostrey		1233								2 34						4 23						6 19
Chelford, for Knutsford..		1240								2 40						4 29	4 51				6 15	6 26
Alderley Edge		1248		1 15						2 48	2 55		3 40			4 37	4 58	5 34			6 26	6 32
Wilmslow	12 5	1254		1 19		1k48	1 53		2 10		3 0		3 45			4 44		5 40		6 0	6 32	
Styal	12 9								2 15				3 49							6 4		
Heald Green	1213								2 19				3 53							6 8		
Gatley ....[Wood	1217								2 23				3 57							6 12		
East Didsbury & Parr's	1220								2 27				4 0							6 15		
Burnage	1223												4 3							6 18		
Mauldeth Road *	1226								2 30				4 6							6 21		
Handforth		1259		1 23							3 5					4 49					6 37	
Cheadle Hulme 529 [526		1 4		1 28							3 10					4 54					6 42	
Stockport ¶ 503, 520, arr		1 10	1 19	1 34	1 42		2 1	2 14		2 59	3 16	3 39		4 18	4 31	5 0	5 10	5 51	6 8		6 48	
Manchester ¶ 503, 505 London Rd. "	12½c	1 23	1 35		1 55	2 5		2 27	2c42	3 15	3 28	3 50	4c17	4 30	4 45	5 15	5 28	6 5	6 23	6c30	7 3	
Oxford Rd. "	1239								2 47				4 23							6 35		
Victoria .. "							2 23	2 53											6 40			

Down.	Week Days—*Continued.*																
Euston Station,	aft	aft	aft	aft	aft	aft	aft	aft	aft	aft		aft	aft	aft	aft	aft	aft
						Via Macclesfield.				Dining Car Express.	To Colne, see pp. 766 & 744.						
404London ....dep.						4 5			4 10	6 5				5 35		8i0	10 0
404Birmingham † ... "	4n55				5 50									7 55	8 40	1015	1125t
458Bristol (Tem. Md.) "	2t20								4t10							7t40	
458Shrewsbury .... "	5 35				5 45				7 22					7 40		1050	mrn
Crewe ....dep.	6 25			6 40	7 18				8 10					9 42	1024	1220	2 0
Sandbach				6 50											1033	1&3	2 8
Holmes Chapel				6 58				7 45							1040		
Goostrey				7 4				7 51							Sat.		
Chelford, for Knutsford..				7 13				7 58					9 40		1049		2 23
Alderley Edge			7 0	7 21				8 5	a				9 48	10 4	1057		
Wilmslow		6 55	7 5	7 26			7 50	8 13		9k18	9 24	9 35	9 54	1010	11 2		
Styal		7 0					7 54					9 40					
Heald Green		7 4					7 58					9 44					
Gatley ....[Wood		7 8					8 2					9 48					
East Didsbury & Parr's		7 12					8 5					9 52					
Burnage							8 8										
Mauldeth Road *		7 15					8 11					9 55					
Handforth			7 10					8 18					9 59		11 7		
Cheadle Hulme 529 [526			7 15					8 23					10 4		1112		
Stockport ¶ 503, 520, arr	6 56		7 21	7 36	7 50	8 1		8 29	8 45		9 33		1010	1022	1117	1253	2 42
Manchester ¶ 503, 505 London Rd. "	7 10	7c25	7 35	7 50	8 5	8 15	8c20	8 42	9 0	9 35		10c5		1038	1130	1 10	3 0
Oxford Rd. "							8 25					1010					
Victoria .. "						8 28					9 55						

For SUNDAY TRAINS, see page 518.

a Stops at 8 32 aft. to set down. *b* Mondays only. **c** Stop to set down on informing Guard at Crewe.
c M. S. J. & A. Platform. *i* Leaves at 8 45 aft. on Saturdays. *k* Stop to set down. *n* Tuesdays and Thursdays.
o Except Sunday nights, 1st and 3rd class. *t* 1st and 3rd class. *u* Leaves at 10 10 mrn. on and after 16th instant.
* Station for Withington. † New Street Station.

July 1910

CREWE, ALDERLEY EDGE, STOCKPORT, and MANCHESTER

August 1940

Miles from Crewe	Down.	Week Days.																				
		aft	aft P	aft	mrn P	mrn SC	mrn SC	mrn	mrn	mrn	mrn	mrn	mrn	mrn	mrn E	mrn	mrn	aft	aft	mrn X	mrn RC	aft S
		TC to Leeds (arr 2 45 mrn)				Mondays only	Except Mondays						TC from Birmingham		TC from Birmingham	TC from Birmingham	TC from London				Via Stoke-on-Trent	
	412London (Euston) ...dep	8 45	8 45	10 50	12V2	1210	1220										8R30			10R0	1020	
	413Birmingham (NewSt.) "	1020	1020	10N55	3V27								6 40		8 30	9 10	9 50			1140		
	Crewe ....dep	1235	1250	2 42	5 40				6 50	7 23	7 45		9 0	9 12	9 58	1050	12 5	1243		1 35		
4⅝	Sandbach	mrn	mrn	mrn					6 58	7 32	7 55		9 9	9 20				1251				
8⅝	Holmes Chapel								7 5	7 40	8 2			9 27				1258				
10⅝	Goostrey								7 10	7 45	8 7			9 32				1 3				
14¼	Chelford, for Knutsford								7 17	7 54	8 14	8 53		9 39				1 10	1S24			
17¼	Alderley Edge				6 4				7 25	8 0	8 20	8 59		9 45				1 16	1S29	1 57		
18⅞	Wilmslow				6 10			7 0	7 34	8 9	8 29	9 3		9 52			1230	1 21	1 35	2 2		2 10
20¼	Handforth							7 3	7 39	8 13	8 33			9 56				1 25				2 18
22⅛	Cheadle Hulme							7 8	7 46	8 19	8 38			10 1				1 30				2 18
25	Stockport 523, 538 ...arr.		1 29	3 15	6 23	3 51	4 2	7 15	7 54	8 26	8 45		9 37	10 8	1032	1124	1242	1 37		2 13	2 18	2 25
—	Manchester (Mayfield) "							7 42				9 35										2 38
30¾	" (London Rd.) "		1 52	3 35	6 43	4 6	4 17		8 8	8 40	9 5		9 51	1022	1048	1138	1257	1 50	2 8	2 28	2 32	

Down.	Week Days—*Continued*																			
	mrn	aft	mrn	aft K	aft	aft	aft RC	aft	aft E	aft X	aft	aft S	E RC	aft C	aft	aft	aft	aft P	aft E	aft S
		TC from Birmingham					Via Stoke-on-Trent; TC London to Colne					TC from London			Via Stoke-on-Trent		TC to Leeds (arr. 2 45 mrn.)			
412London (Euston) ...dep.	10 40		1150	1 10			2 50	2R40			4 10	5R30	5 40	5E30			8 45	8 45	1050	1155
413Birmingham (NewSt) "		2 0					4 0	4 0		5 45		5 55		5 55	6 30		1020	1020	1055	1055
Crewe ....dep	2 45	3 50	4 18	5 5		5 48		6 30		7 25	7 40	8 55		9 6		9 45	1235	1250	2 42	3 25
Sandbach	2 53		4 35			5 58					7 48					9 53				SC
Holmes Chapel	3 0		4 42	5 18		6 3					7 55					10 0				
Goostrey	3 5		4 47			6 8					8 0					10 5				
Chelford, for Knutsford	3 12		4 54			6 15			7 2		8 7			9Z26		1012				
Alderley Edge	3 18		5 0	5 36		6 21			7 7		8 13			9 32		1018				
Wilmslow	3 23		5†24	5 41	5 49	6 26		6 57	7 12	7 49	8 18	9 18	9 18	9 37		1023				
Handforth	3 27				5 52	6 30			7 16		8 22					1027				
Cheadle Hulme	3 32				5 57	6 35			7 21		8 27				1022	1032				
Stockport 523, 538 ...arr.	3 39	4 24		5 54	6 4	6 42	6 57	7 8	7 28	8 0	8 34	9 28	9 28	9 47	1029	1039		1Y29	3 15	3 58
Manchester (Mayfield) "																				
(London Rd.) "	3 53	4 40	5 57	6 8	6 27	7 2	7 11	7 23	7 55	8 13	8 47	9 42	9 42	10 2	1042	1055		1Y52	3 35	4 13

Down.					Sundays.													
	aft Sat.	P Sat.	aft Sat.	aft Sat.	mrn P	mrn	mrn	mrn X	mrn	aft C	aft	aft X	aft X	aft	aft RC	aft	aft C	aft
	TC to Leeds (arr 2 45 mrn)						TC from Birmingham	Via Stoke-on-Trent	TC from London		TC from London	Via Stoke-on-Trent				TC to Leeds (arr. 2 45 mrn.)		
412London (Euston) ...dep.	8 45	8 45	1155		12 2				10R20	1 10	2 40				5 30	8 45	8 45	1055
413Birmingham (NewSt.) "	1020	1020	1055	1055	3 15		9 10	9 40	11 40			4 50	5 45		6 50	1020	1020	1115
Crewe ....dep.	1235	1250	3 25	4 25	5 40	8 50	1050		1 51	5 5	6 15		7 25	7 40	9 0	1235	1250	2 42
Sandbach	mrn	mrn	SC	mrn		8 58								7 48				
Holmes Chapel						9 5								7 55				
Goostrey						9 10								8 0				
Chelford for Knutsford						9 17								8 7				
Alderley Edge					6 4	9 23				5 33				8 13				
Wilmslow					6 10	9 28				5 38			7 49	8 18	9 27			
Handforth						9 32								8 22				
Cheadle Hulme						9 37		1242				7 44		8 27				
Stockport 523, 538 ...arr.		1 24	3 58	5 3	6 23	9 44	1126	1249	2 24	5 49	6 48	7 51	8 9	8 34	9 39		1 29	3 15
Manchester (Mayfield) "																		
" (London Rd.) "		1 47	4 13	5 23	6 43	10 1	1140	1 5	2 38	6 5	7 3	8 10	8 13	8 47	9 54		1 52	3 35

C Thro Carrs. from Cardiff. E or E Except Sats. K Thro Carrs. from Paignton and Cardiff. N Dep. 11 15 aft on Suns.
P Thro Carrs. from Penzance. R Restaurant Car, London to Crewe. RC Restaurant Car, London to Manchester. S or S Sats. only.
SC 1st and 3rd class Sleeping accommodation, London to Manchester. † Arr. 5 7 aft. TC Thro Carrs. U Dep. 11 55 aft on Suns.
V Dep 2 59 mrn on Mondays X Through Carriages from Birmingham. Y 5 mins. earlier on Sun. morns.
Z Stops to set down only from Stations beyond Crewe on notice being given to Guard at Crewe.

CREWE

III. The 1911 map at 6ins to 1 mile has the 1837 GJR main line running straight from top to bottom. Its branch to Chester is on the left and the M&BR route to Manchester is top right. Lower right is the Kidsgrove line and lower left is the Shrewsbury route. Between these junctions is Crewe South engine shed, which was coded 5B by BR and was in use from 1897 to 1967. The first engine shed was northwest of the station and was in use from 1839 until 1851. It was demolished to allow further expansion of the station. The three adjacent sheds became known as Crewe North. These and their successors, together with Crewe Works are featured in our *Stafford to Chester* album (pictures 68-80). The junction beyond the lower border and South Shed are in pictures 42-47 in that album. The area to the left of them is shown in pictures 90-94 in *Shrewsbury to Crewe*. The population was around 200 in the 1830s and rose to 4571 by 1851, 17,810 in 1861 and was 67,683 in 2001, the stimulus being the railway growth. Congestion necessitated a bypass: the "Independent Lines" are to the left of the station and they gave double track links to all three routes north from the station. They were electrified with difficulty, owing to tunnels. They were still used for freight traffic in 2014.

1. We look north over the first curve on the route to Manchester, in 1898. The workshop area was for the permanent way department and beyond it is a small gasworks, which provided the railway's requirements for carriage lighting and kitchen car fuel. The elderly rolling stock may have been recently retired. Initially, there was a gate here over the single line of the M&BR, which was laid to 4ft 9ins gauge. (R.M.Casserley coll.)

2. An express from Manchester is passing over North Junction in about 1922 and it largely obscures the curve seen in the last photograph. Featured is "Precursor" class no. 1395 *Harbinger*. The route to Chester was originally 4ft 8¾ins gauge, to give "more play". Thus Crewe had three gauges initially. (R.S.Carpenter coll.)

3. North Junction signal box is on the left of the previous picture and is seen in 1936, when it had 266 miniature levers. The previous box had 155 tall levers and was in use from 1876 to 1906. A flat-roofed LMS box with 214 small levers served here from 1940 until 1985. The box seen became part of the Crewe Heritage Centre. (R.S.Carpenter coll.)

4. Shunting the sidings, seen in picture no. 1, on 7th May 1949 is class 4P 4-4-0 no. 41167. The bridge is over the river from which water was extracted for the works and the locomotives. A reservoir was built nearby. (H.C.Casserley)

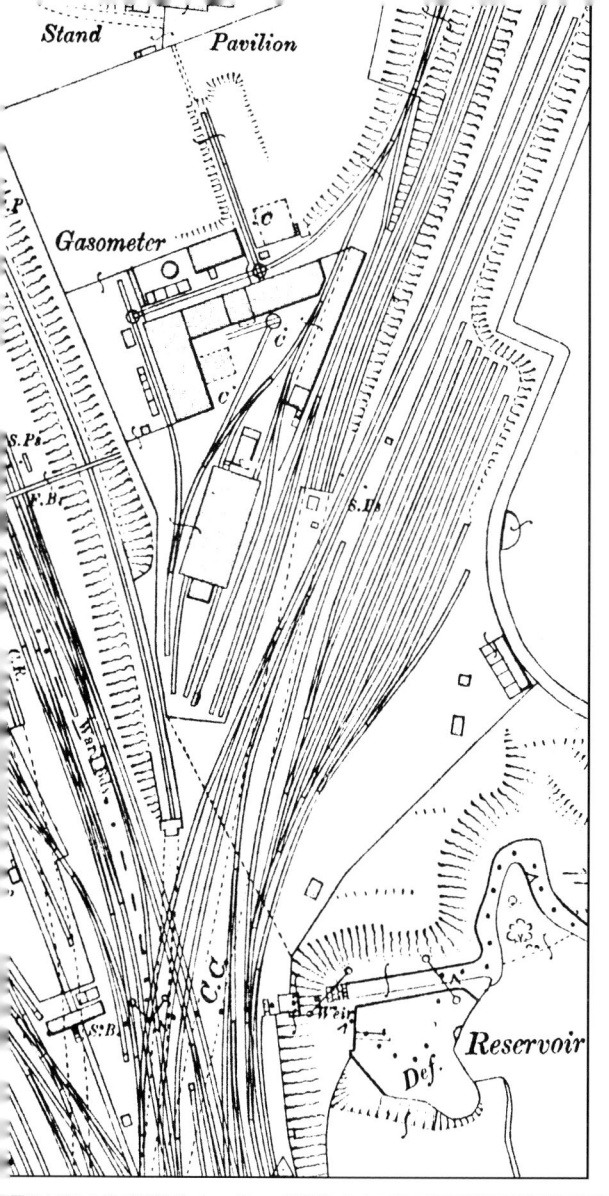

IV. The Grand Junction's gasworks of 1843 was beside the Coppenhall Brook, just west of where Crewe North engine shed was later built. A zig-zag siding brought in the coal but, as the locomotive shed expanded westward, the necessary embankment buried the gasworks. Gas was made on a better site near the New Works from about 1884. The replacement gasworks was a mile to the west, between Victoria Avenue and the Valley Brook. Works shunters came under Victoria Avenue pushing coal wagons for the gasworks, and charged up an incline to reach the high-level bunkers inside the Retort House. At nationalisation, British Railways became the gas supplier to Crewe and not until 1st January 1952 did they pass the business to the North Western Gas Board. Once road access had been made, Yorkshire coal by rail quickly yielded to North Staffordshire coal by lorry, with considerable savings. Coal itself gave way to naphtha feedstock in about 1960. Although the railway took no interest in the modernised gasworks, Crewe Works consumed much more gas than ever before. The small gasworks shown on this 1908 survey is described in caption 1. Meandering lower right is the Valley Brook, which provided the original water supply for the GJR. The northern tunnel mouth of the Manchester Independent Lines can be found a little above centre. The other two tunnels also have dotted lines.

5. Class 5 4-6-0 no. 44686 arrives on 29th May 1952 with the northbound "Pines Express" from Bournemouth. Included is "B" Box, which was in use until 1st April 1960. Starting with only two platforms, the station had growth phases in 1867 and 1887, plus major changes in 1903-06. (R.S.Carpenter coll.)

6.   The hotel was built in the Jacobean style and opened in 1837. It was acquired by the LNWR in 1864 and provided a suitable backdrop for no. 86427 *The Industrial Society* with the 16.00 Euston to Manchester on 15th June 1988. (T.Heavyside)

7.   It is 1st October 1994 and we are close to the Crewe Arms, which was converted to offices. Crewe to Manchester local trains generally used platform 1, there being no north facing bay on the up side of the station. Here though, no. 87008 has brought empty stock from Longsight Depot and has run round to continue to Preston to take up a southbound working. (A.C.Hartless)

8. Preserved class 55s were unusual visitors to Crewe. Present on 15th May 1999 were nos 55009 *Alycidon* and 55019 *Royal Highland Fusilier*. The white signal box in the distance is part of the Crewe Heritage Centre, which is in the divergence of the Chester and Warrington lines. (P.Jones)

9. There was a rare opportunity to survey the north end of the station on 15th May 2013, as "The Cathedrals Explorer" reversed at platform 12. Passengers from London travelled via Exeter, Cardiff, Minffordd, Caernarfon, Preston, Hexham, Whitby and Malton. There were a few road links, but haulage was mostly with steam; the operator was Steam Dreams. (V.Mitchell)

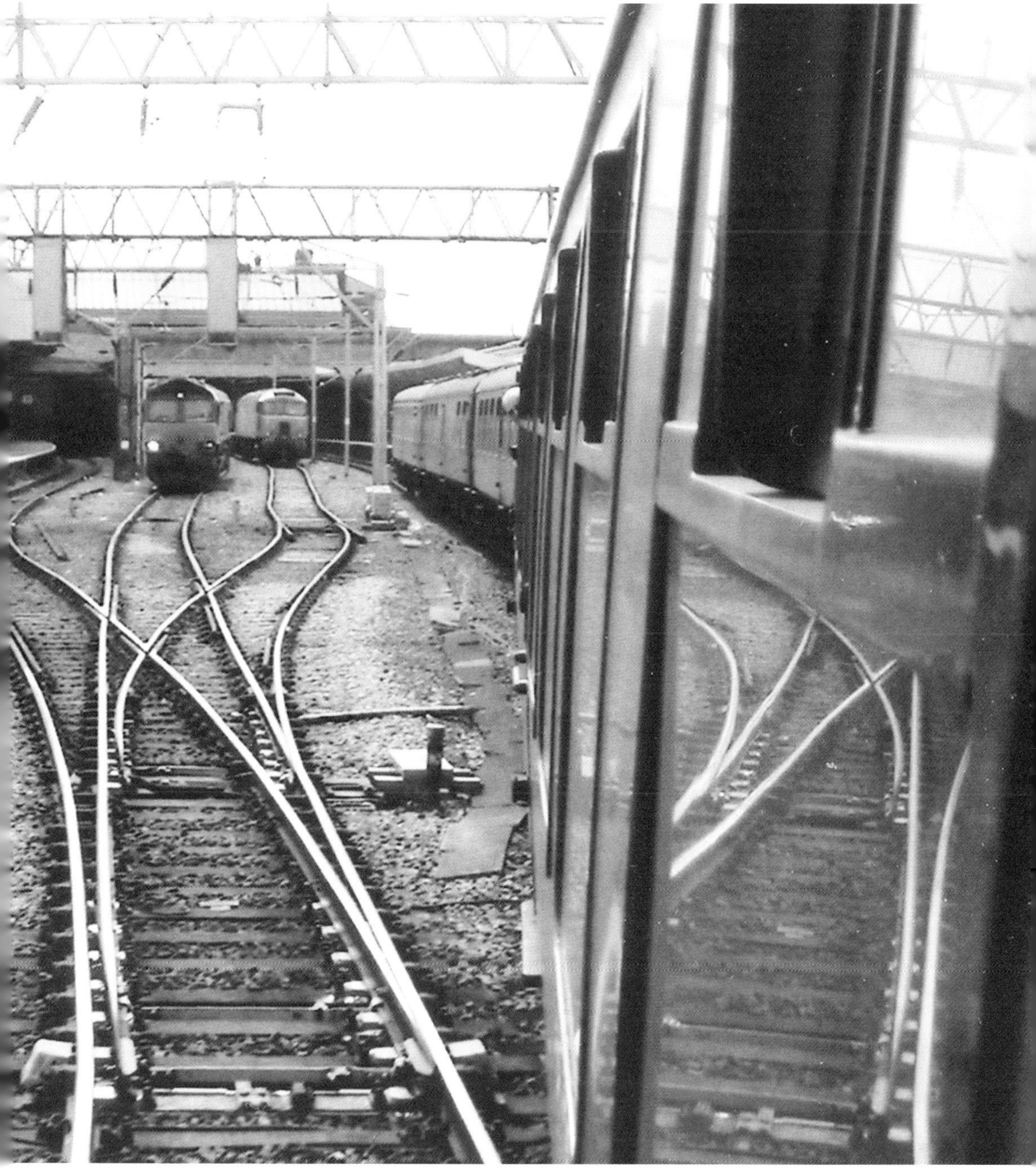

SANDBACH

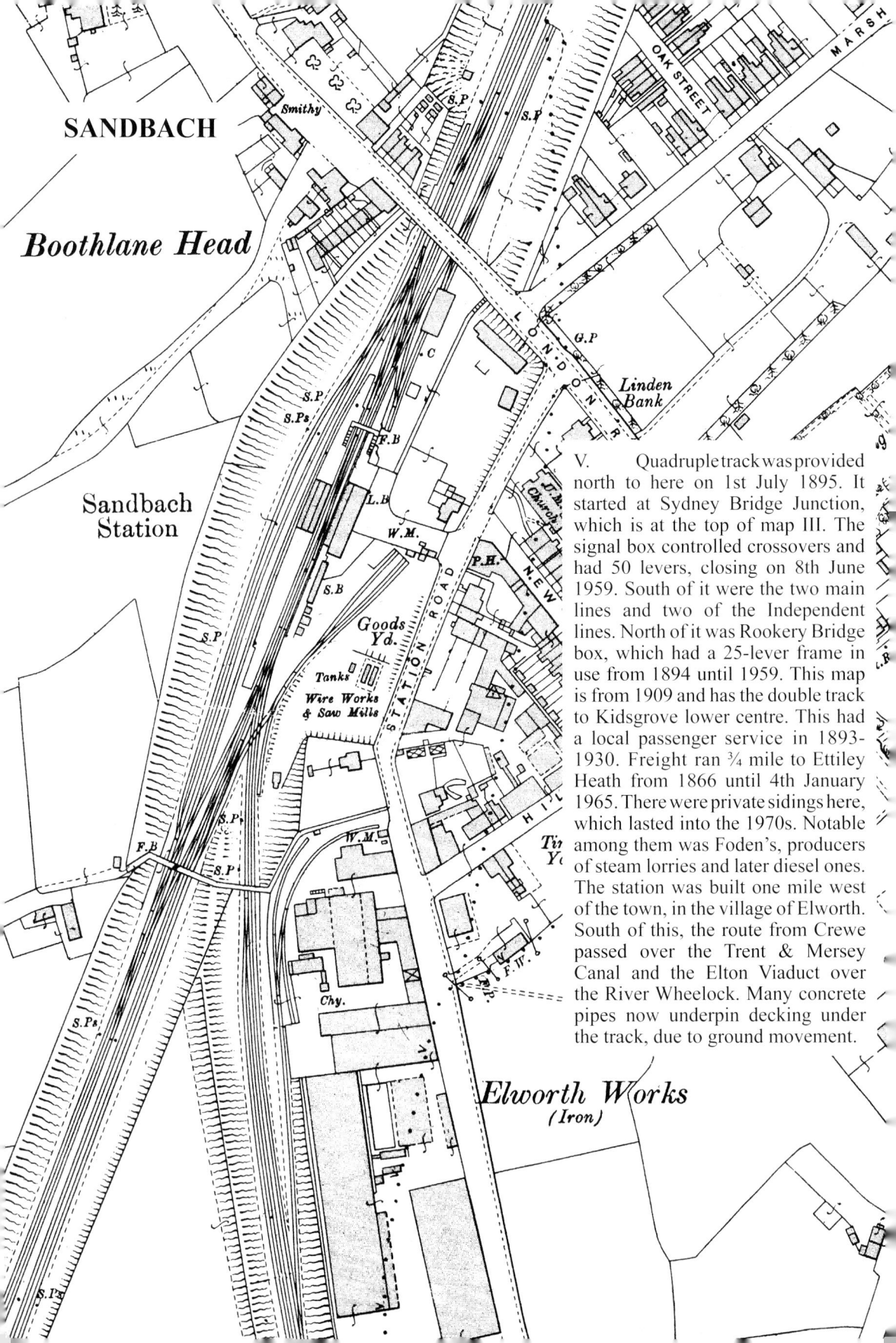

Boothlane Head

Sandbach Station

Elworth Works (Iron)

V. Quadruple track was provided north to here on 1st July 1895. It started at Sydney Bridge Junction, which is at the top of map III. The signal box controlled crossovers and had 50 levers, closing on 8th June 1959. South of it were the two main lines and two of the Independent lines. North of it was Rookery Bridge box, which had a 25-lever frame in use from 1894 until 1959. This map is from 1909 and has the double track to Kidsgrove lower centre. This had a local passenger service in 1893-1930. Freight ran ¾ mile to Ettiley Heath from 1866 until 4th January 1965. There were private sidings here, which lasted into the 1970s. Notable among them was Foden's, producers of steam lorries and later diesel ones. The station was built one mile west of the town, in the village of Elworth. South of this, the route from Crewe passed over the Trent & Mersey Canal and the Elton Viaduct over the River Wheelock. Many concrete pipes now underpin decking under the track, due to ground movement.

10. This postcard shows more sidings than the map and so must post-date it. The 10-ton crane is included, as is the 1894 signal box. It had 108 levers and was working until 8th June 1959. It was replaced by a power box, which lasted until 19th June 2006, when Manchester South Signalling Centre took control. (Lens of Sutton coll.)

11. The cattle pens are included in this view of a down express speeding through on 21st March 1957, headed by class 5 4-6-0 no. 45289. The district was extensively worked for salt, which resulted in much ground settlement and consequent speed restrictions. Most expresses were later routed via Macclesfield. (Bentley coll.)

12. A northward view from 6th June 1958 has a class 9F 2-10-0 heading a wiring train. Being freight only, the Kidsgrove branch is fitted with catch points. The goods yard was in use until 9th February 1967. (Bentley coll.)

13. The station was completely rebuilt with flat-roofed structures at the time of electrification. An LCGB special train was worked by class 2 2-6-2T no. 41286 on 5th February 1966. (D.K.Jones)

14.   We are north of the station on 15th June 1988 as no. 37427 *Bont y Bermo* works the 14.00 Cardiff to Manchester Piccadilly service. On the right are the lines towards Middlewich which were electrified for only ½ mile. Unclear in the distance is the power box. (T.Heavyside)

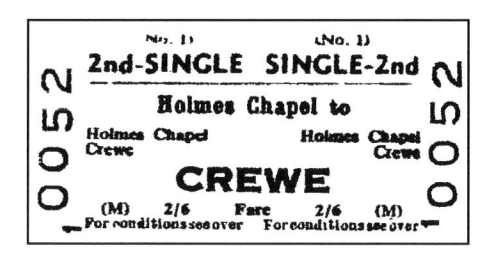

Northwich Branch
SOUTH OF MIDDLEWICH

15.   Running south on 15th June 1988 are nos 20160 and 20177 with Merry-Go-Round stock. They have just reached the overhead lines. (T.Heavyside)

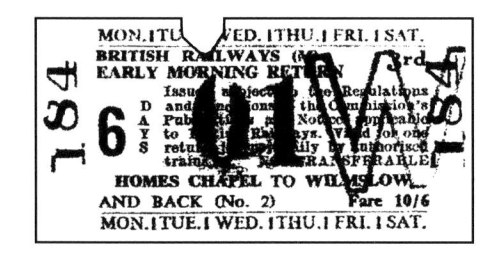

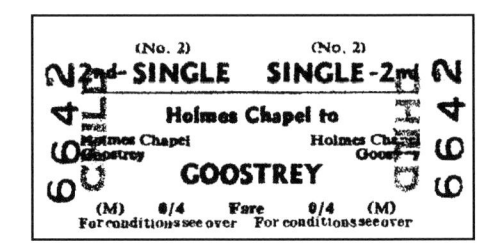

16.   The Murgatroyd's chemical plant at Sandbach went through several changes of ownership, first to BP, then Hays Chemicals and finally Albion Chemicals. Its last rail traffic was hydrochloric acid, which was conveyed to the Roche Pharmaceuticals plant at Dalry. This flow ceased in early 2007. Previous traffic handled at Sandbach had included chlorine and nitric acid. Resident pilot locomotive no. 08523, on hire from RT Rail, shunts six purged hydrochloric acid tanks in the terminal on 14th February 2007, the last day of rail operations on the site. (P.D.Shannon)

17.   EWS locomotive no. 66100 waits in the Albion Chemicals terminal at Sandbach on the same day, ready to form the last ever trip working from Sandbach to Warrington. On this occasion the train would convey six purged hydrochloric acid tanks destined for storage at Shirebrook. This kind of wagonload freight operation involving the use of a shunting locomotive was already an anachronism by 2007. (P.D.Shannon)

18.   We are four miles south of Middlewich and no. 31516 propels three empty salt hoppers into the British Salt terminal on 2nd May 1992, having worked the three times weekly Railfreight Distribution chemicals trip from Warrington. A single empty tank wagon for Sandbach has been temporarily left on the main running line. After exchanging the empty salt hoppers for loaded wagons, the class 31 will couple up again to the empty tank wagon and continue to Sandbach. The salt was bound for the Roche Pharmaceuticals factory at Dalry, a flow that would continue to move by rail until 2001. The British Salt siding was retained after that date for a possible flow of brine from Northwich, but as things turned out the brine traffic never got beyond the trial stage and the siding was abandoned. (P.D.Shannon)

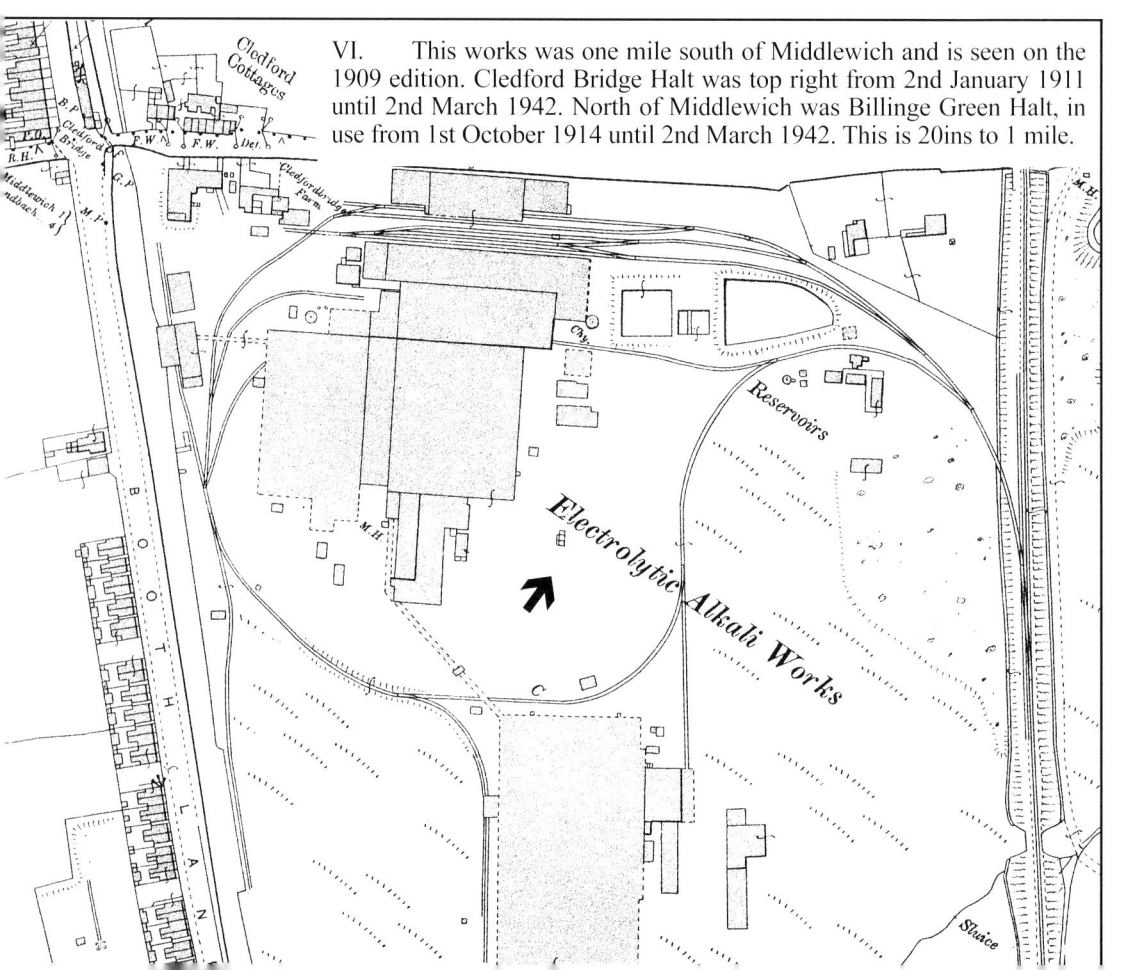

VI.   This works was one mile south of Middlewich and is seen on the 1909 edition. Cledford Bridge Halt was top right from 2nd January 1911 until 2nd March 1942. North of Middlewich was Billinge Green Halt, in use from 1st October 1914 until 2nd March 1942. This is 20ins to 1 mile.

MIDDLEWICH

VII. The town was one of the oldest working salt in England and there is much evidence of it on this 1909 map at 20ins to 1 mile. Silk and Cheshire Cheese were other notable products.

19. Looking north from the road bridge in about 1960, we see the goods yard, which seems busy. It closed on 27th November 1967 and had served four coal merchants. Local passengers were carried between 1st July 1868 and 4th January 1960. (Lens of Sutton coll.)

20. A southward panorama in 1965 shows that the lamps have been changed. The line was retained as a diversionary route and was very busy during the electrification works. (Stations UK)

21. The train seen in picture 13 stops to take water. Push-pull sets had been used regularly on the route and this one was valuable on the tour, owing to the many reversals. The journey had to be repeated a week later due to demand. (D.K.Jones)

NORTH OF MIDDLEWICH

22. No. 31516 takes the south to west curve at Northwich with the Railfreight Distribution chemicals trip from Sandbach to Warrington Arpley on 2nd May 1992. The load comprises salt hoppers from Middlewich to Dalry and caustic soda tanks from Sandbach to Dalry. The line between Middlewich and Northwich was temporarily closed one week after the date of this photograph and the chemicals train was rerouted for a time via Crewe. A single line was retained for diversions. The two northern junctions of the triangular junction, together with Northwich can be seen in our *Chester to Manchester* album. (P.D.Shannon)

HOLMES CHAPEL

VIII. The 1909 survey includes an unusually short siding to the crane, which is simply marked C. It was rated at 5 tons. To the south was Bradwell signal box, from 1873 to 1942.

23. A northward view in 1948 includes the cattle dock beyond the goods shed. Further north, a siding for Wallpapers Manufacturers Ltd was listed in 1938. The 1902 signal box had 25 levers and functioned until 8th June 1959.
(Stations UK)

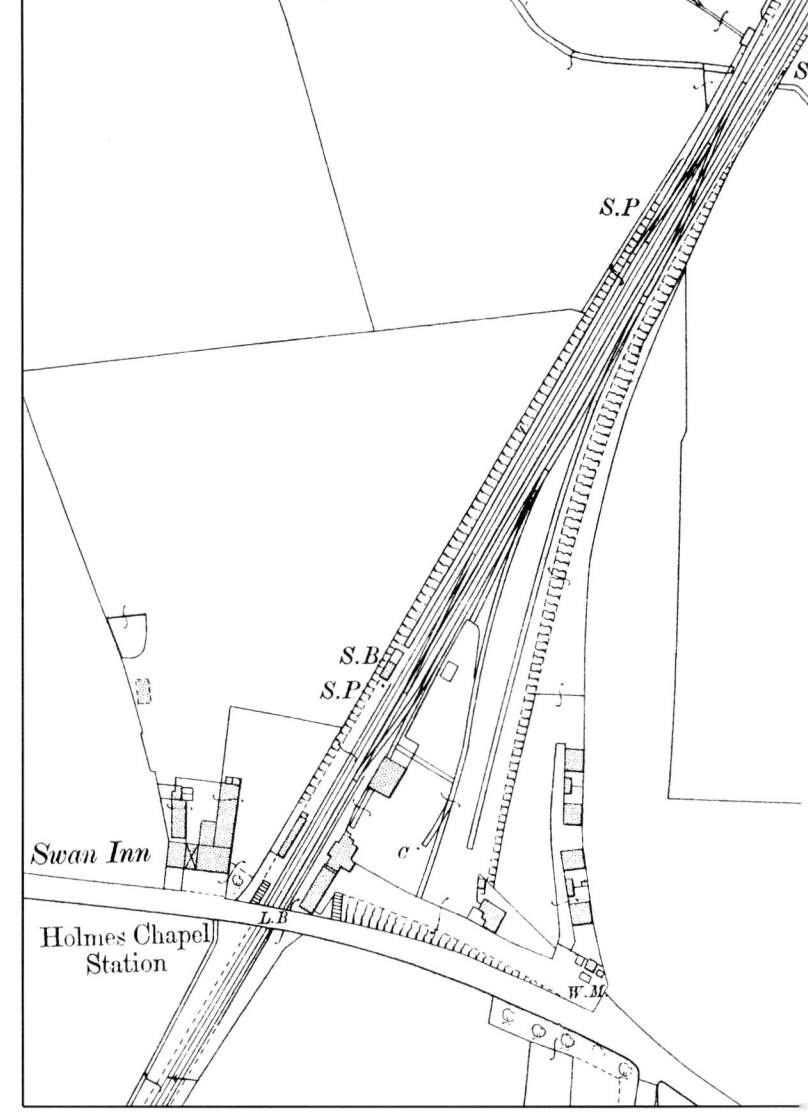

24. Featureless buildings arrived with the advent of electrification and are seen from the north in 1964. Fisons built a large pharmaceutical works further south. (Stations UK)

25. No. 66730 *Whitemoor* is running from Tilbury Docks, east of London, to Trafford Park, west of Manchester, on 25th June 2013. It will soon pass over Dane Viaduct, which has 23 arches and is 105ft high. (A.C.Hartless)

GOOSTREY

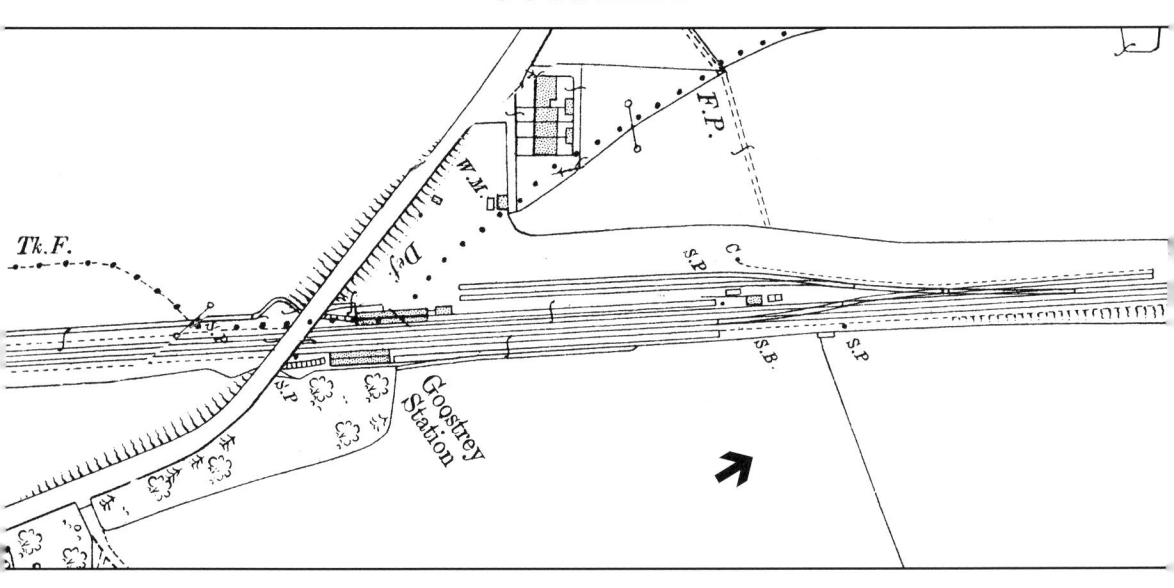

IX. The 1909 edition has a 5-ton crane showing and a weighing machine for road vehicles marked W.M. The cottages are for railway workers. The goods yard closed on 2nd November 1964.

26. A 1948 record includes the 1891 20-lever signal box, which was replaced by a flat-roofed one in 1954. It had 30 levers and was one of a pair intended to serve a large fuel depot. The second one was never used; the first became a ground frame in June 1959 and closed in January 1988. (Stations UK)

27. Photographed on 23rd November 2006, the station was a latecomer, not opening until 1st September 1891. No. 323236 is working the 12.00 Crewe to Manchester Piccadilly and is under the bridge rebuilt to accept the wiring. The up building was reprofiled, as well. (A.C.Hartless)

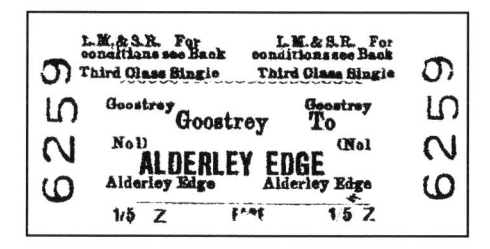

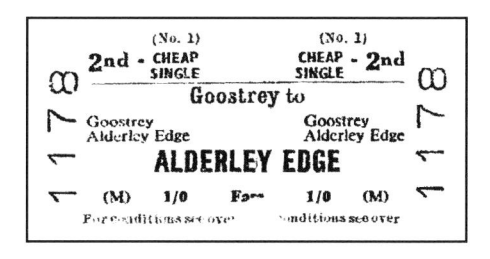

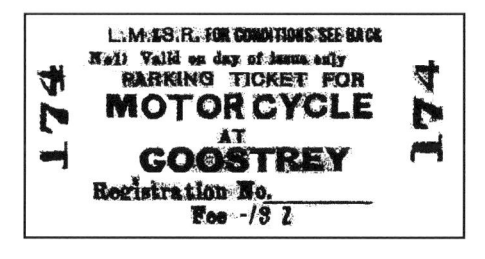

CHELFORD

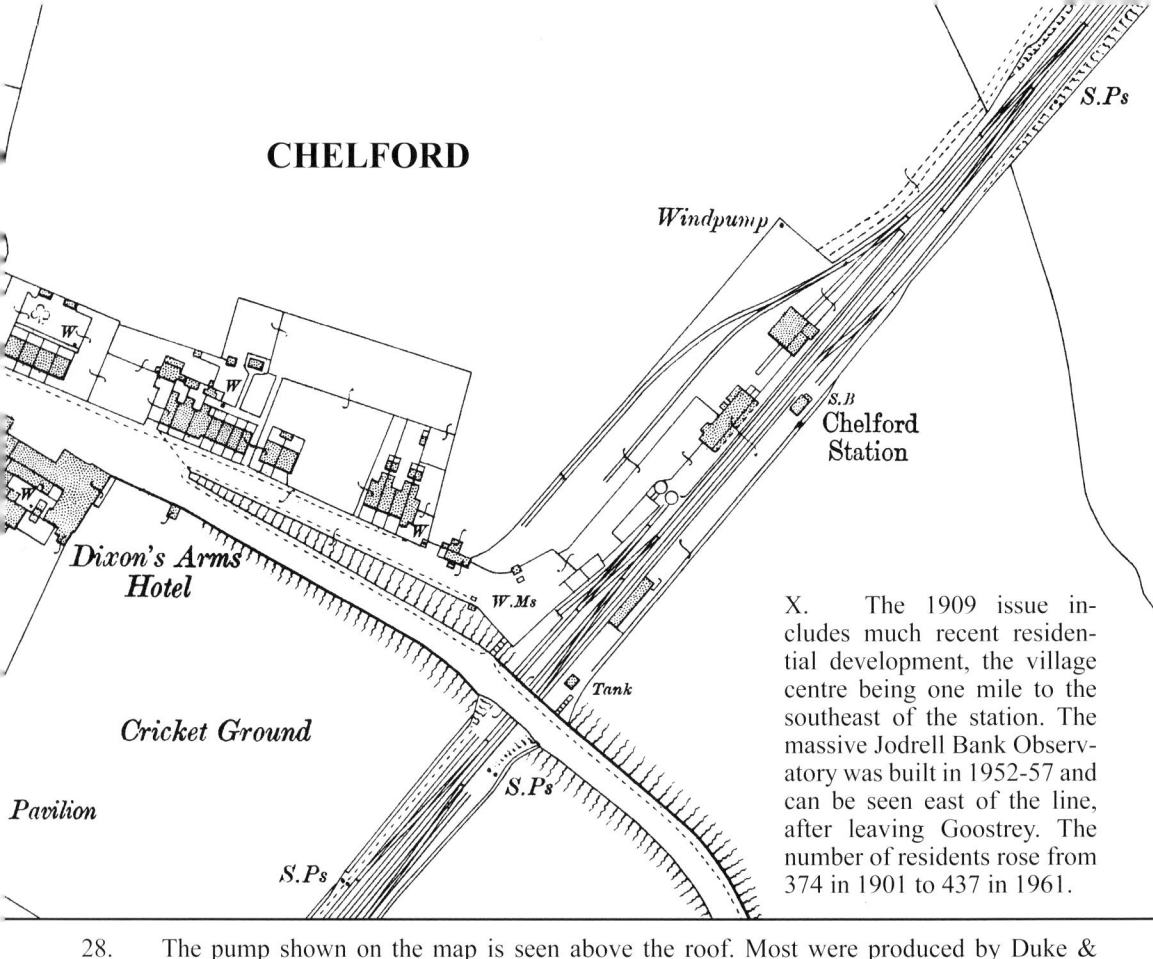

X. The 1909 issue includes much recent residential development, the village centre being one mile to the southeast of the station. The massive Jodrell Bank Observatory was built in 1952-57 and can be seen east of the line, after leaving Goostrey. The number of residents rose from 374 in 1901 to 437 in 1961.

28. The pump shown on the map is seen above the roof. Most were produced by Duke & Ockenden in Littlehampton. One of the two wagon turntables is included in this poor but interesting record. (Lens of Sutton coll.)

29. From around 1930, this view shows more clearly the gap in the up platform, which was for the benefit of milk churns rather than passengers. Trucks and pens for the frustration of cattle are in the left foreground. Chelford Sidings box opened in the distance in 1942 to serve a military fuel depot. It was on the east side of the line and had 55 levers. It was used for shunting only from 29th June 1959 until closure on 30th April 1968. (Stations UK)

30. Looking south in 1955, we see continuity of the up platform. Milk traffic was lost that year due to a strike on the railways. The goods yard continued in use until 4th May 1970. This signal box had 37 levers and the one further south (Chelford Loop) had 20. Both were in use from 1885 until 29th June 1959. (Stations UK)

31. This photographer stated on 24th August 1992: class 304 EMUs worked the local services from electrification for over thirty years. Here no. 304004, reduced to three cars, arrives with the 12.43 Crewe - Deansgate. Beyond the bridge can be seen the points for the up Chelford loop, the down to up trailing crossover, and the down Chelford loop. The downside ticket office and shelter has all the charm of a detention block. (A.C.Hartless)

ALDERLEY EDGE

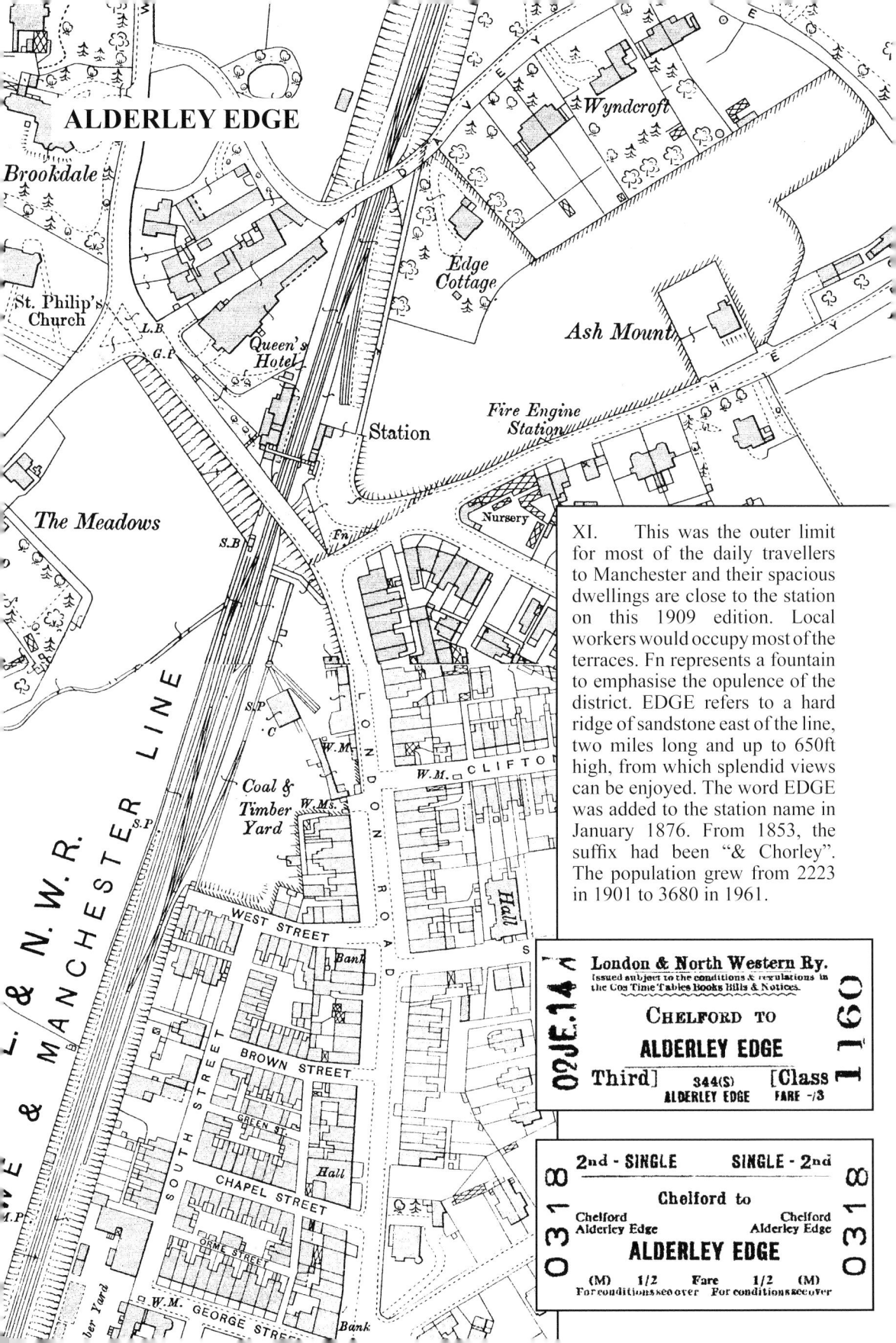

XI. This was the outer limit for most of the daily travellers to Manchester and their spacious dwellings are close to the station on this 1909 edition. Local workers would occupy most of the terraces. Fn represents a fountain to emphasise the opulence of the district. EDGE refers to a hard ridge of sandstone east of the line, two miles long and up to 650ft high, from which splendid views can be enjoyed. The word EDGE was added to the station name in January 1876. From 1853, the suffix had been "& Chorley". The population grew from 2223 in 1901 to 3680 in 1961.

London & North Western Ry.
Issued subject to the conditions & regulations in the Coy Time Tables Books Bills & Notices.

CHELFORD TO
ALDERLEY EDGE

Third]   344(S)   [Class
         ALDERLEY EDGE   FARE -/3

02JE.14   1160

2nd - SINGLE   SINGLE - 2nd
Chelford to
Chelford   Chelford
Alderley Edge   Alderley Edge
ALDERLEY EDGE
(M)   1/2   Fare   1/2   (M)
For conditions see over   For conditions see over

0318   0318

32. This early postcard predates the banning of ballast on top of sleepers. Items of note are the low height of the platforms and the great height of the gentlemens' ventilator and the lamp posts.
(Lens of Sutton coll.)

33. This card was postmarked 1914 and includes vans at the end loading dock, where the carriages of the wealthy would be unloaded from flat wagons by horses. Three stand awaiting passengers and are on the cobbled area used to receive their prolific droppings. The side of the Queen's Hotel is in the background.
(P.Laming coll.)

34. The 20-lever signal box of about 1870 is seen on 26th April 1955. It was in use until 29th June 1959, but the adjacent siding continued to be used for terminating trains.
(H.F.Wheeller/
R.S.Carpenter coll.)

35. A view from the 1960s reveals the great length of the gantries required to span both canopies and tracks. The lattice steel footbridge was replaced by a precast concrete structure. (Lens of Sutton coll.)

36. These concrete spans were erected at the north end of the station to carry a local road. No. 005 is running in from Manchester on 5th April 1980, while working an Altrincham to Crewe service. (T.Heavyside)

37. Two reversing sidings were provided and the crossover in the previous picture gave access to the down one. No. 304042 is about to pass under the rebuilt stone bridge on 1st August 1983, forming the 14.22 Crewe to Altrincham. In the siding waits no. 304027 ready to return to Manchester Piccadilly at 15.04. (A.C.Hartless)

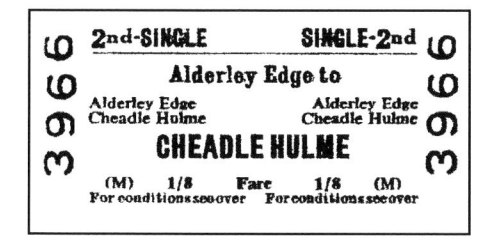

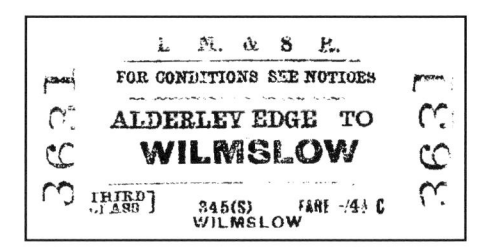

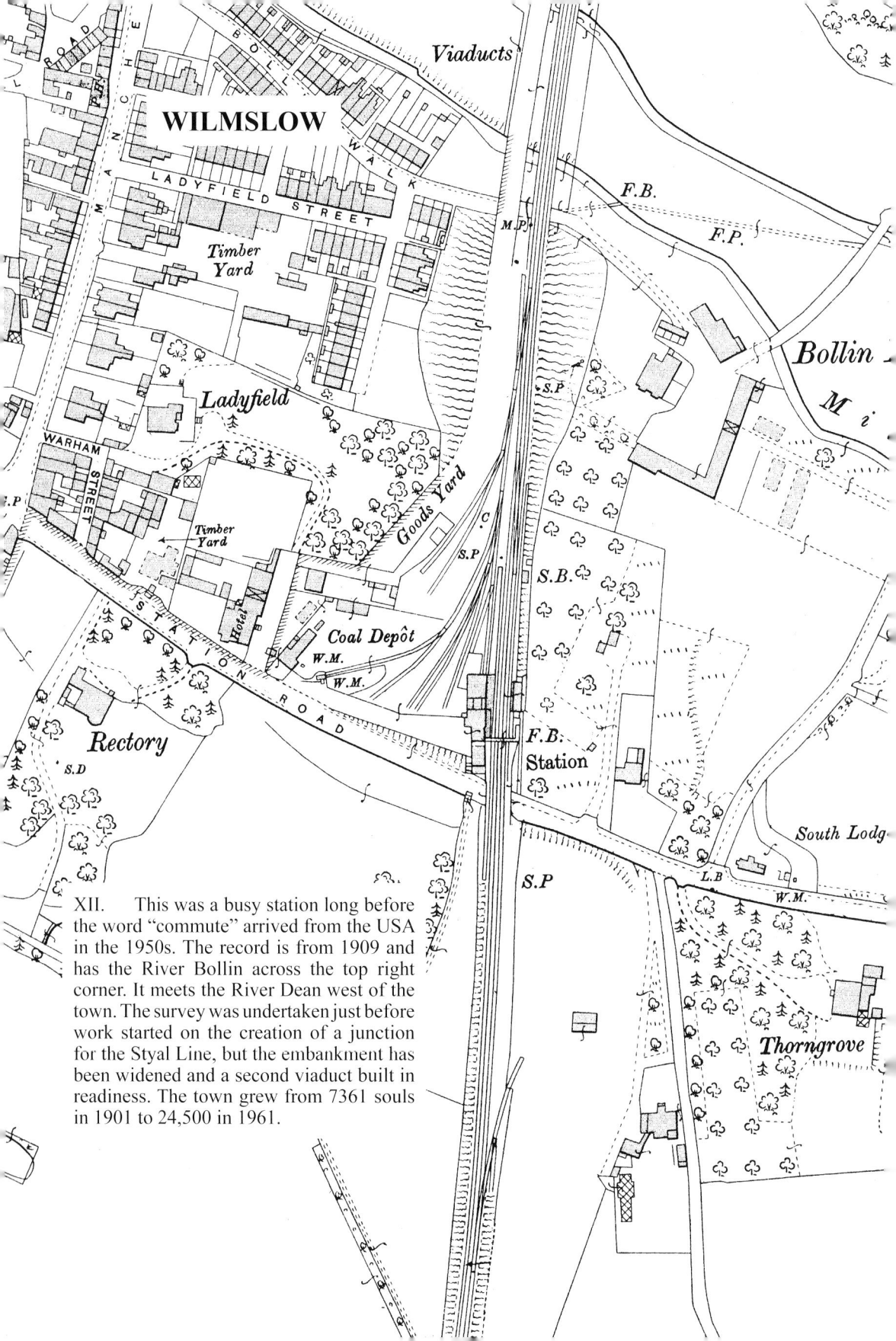

XII. This was a busy station long before the word "commute" arrived from the USA in the 1950s. The record is from 1909 and has the River Bollin across the top right corner. It meets the River Dean west of the town. The survey was undertaken just before work started on the creation of a junction for the Styal Line, but the embankment has been widened and a second viaduct built in readiness. The town grew from 7361 souls in 1901 to 24,500 in 1961.

38.   Large gas mantles are evident as we note that the platform above Station Road is also gas lit. Four cabs await fares as we examine the extensive cobbles and their condition. (Lens of Sutton coll.)

39.   A totally new station was available from 1909, it having four platforms instead of two and a subway instead of a footbridge. This is a northward view in about 1930. (Stations UK)

40. A southward shot from the 1960s has the Styal Line platforms on the right and the tall tower of the Wilmslow Power Signal Box at the end of the centre one. It came into use on 29th June 1959, replacing a 66-lever box opened in 1908. (Lens of Sutton coll.)

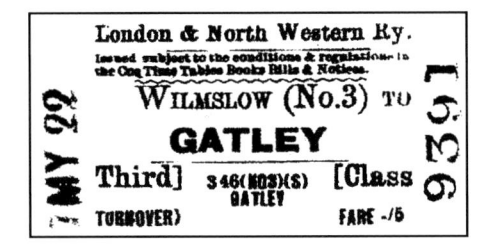

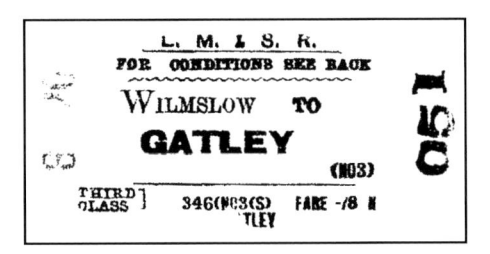

41. A Euston to Manchester express is on the junction for the Styal Line on 18th June 1960. It is seen from the new box, as is the goods yard which was on the opposite side of the running lines from the one on the map. Freight traffic ceased on 2nd May 1970. (E.Wilmshurst)

42. It is 5th April 1980 and no. 304029 is working from Altrincham to Alderley Edge. The massive box raised much local objection, but remained in use until 19th June 2006. (T.Heavyside)

Styal Line

XIII. The Styal Line bypasses Stockport and was chosen to be the pilot line for the new electrification system in 1959. Installation techniques and all types of equipment were tried and tested here, without interfering with main line traffic. All aspects of training were also undertaken on the route. (British Railways)

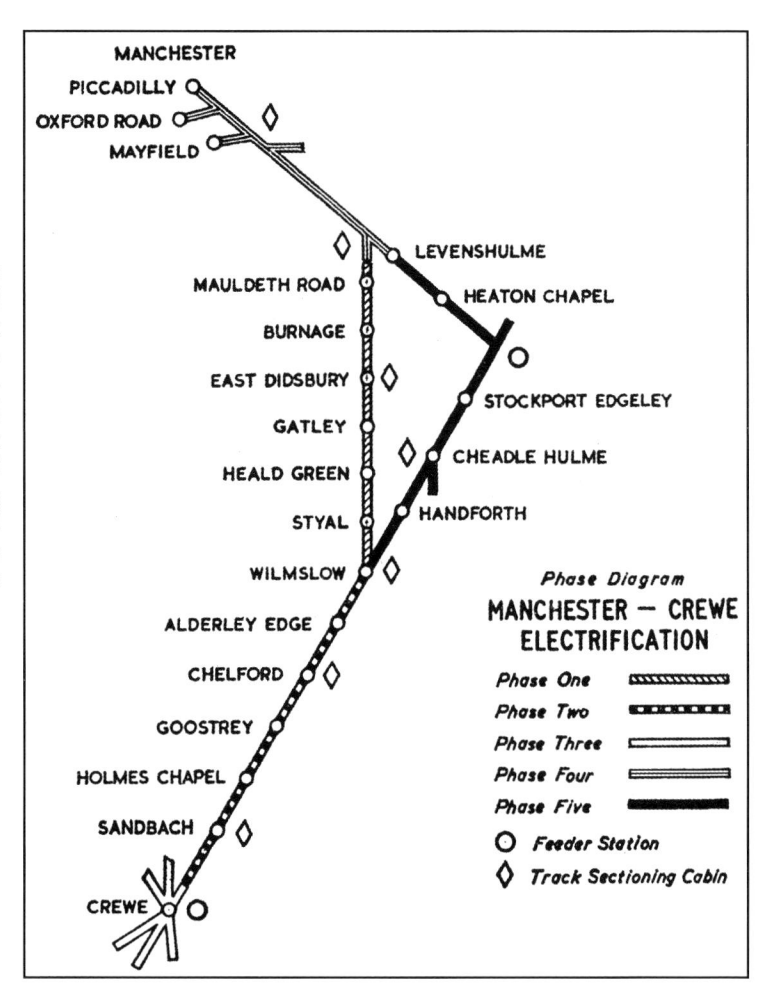

STYAL

XIV. The goods yard had a 5-ton crane and closed on 4th November 1963. The station was staffed part time only from 25th April 1967. On leaving Wilmslow, the line runs over Bollin Viaduct, which has eleven arches and is 60ft high.

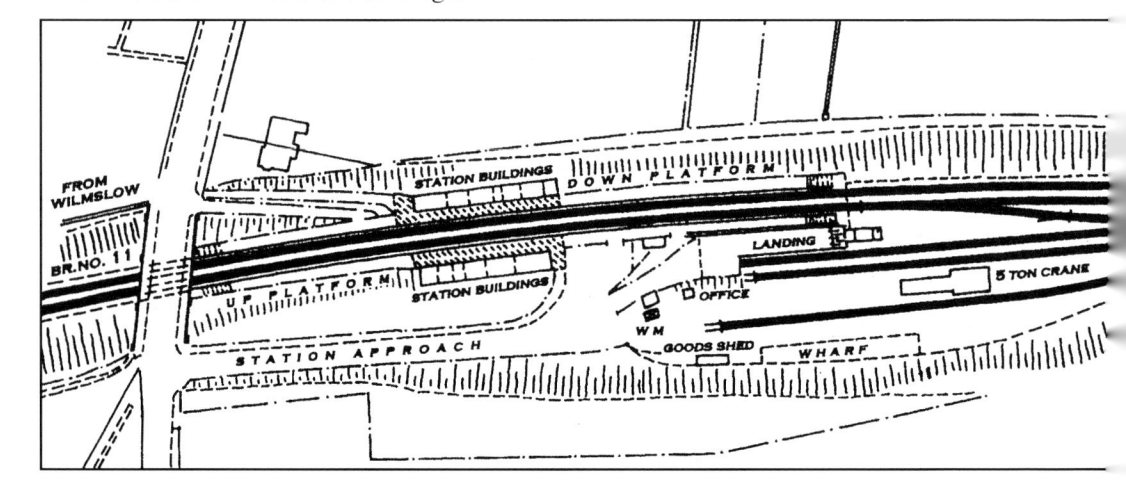

43. A north view at the time of opening has the signal box in the distance and the lamp room nearer to the up buildings. One man was noted for having spent his entire career of 50 years here. (A.Dudman coll.)

44. Working the 13.50 Altrincham to Alderley Edge on 11th May 1985 is EMU no. 304016. The original buildings had been destroyed in 1960 in favour of the featureless flat-pack type. The track for half mile north of Wilmslow had to be lowered by up to 4ft, due to bridges that could not be raised for the wires. (T.Heavyside)

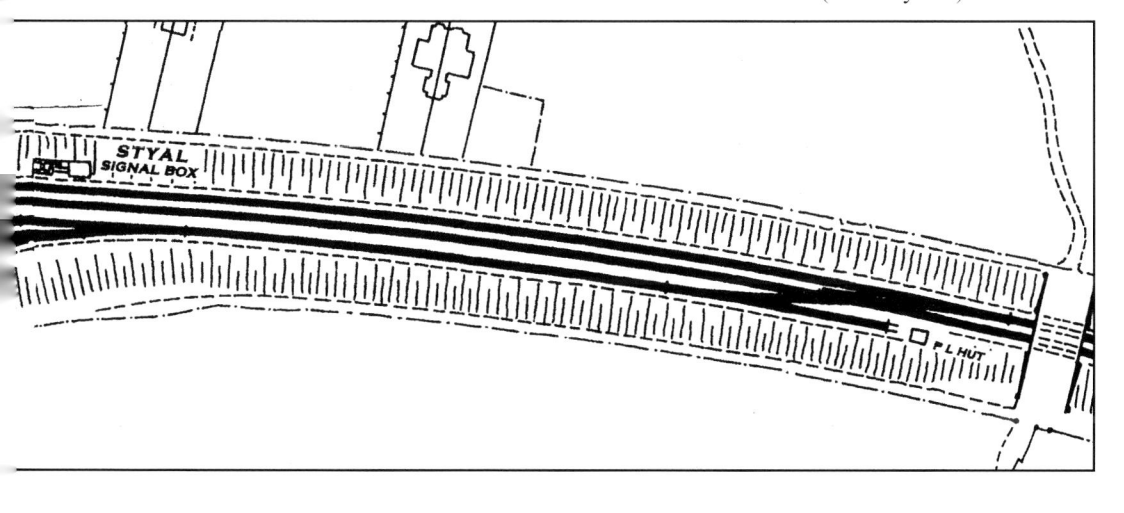

MANCHESTER AIRPORT

45. The branch terminus was built between Terminals 1 and 2. It was connected to the former by a covered travellator and the latter by a bus service. The first passenger trains into the station on opening day on 30th March 1993 were class 150/1 Sprinter no. 150138 and class 158 Regional Express no. 158809, having emanated from Blackpool North and Scarborough, respectively. They are seen above, near the buffer stops. (B.Morrison)

XV. Branch diagram after the completion of the triangle in 1996 and the third platform in 2008. A fourth one was announced in 2012.

46. In newly-applied Manchester Airport livery, Regional Railways' no. 309624 arrives at Manchester Airport station on 21st May 1996, to form the 14.10 special to Birmingham New Street. The outline of the spectacular entrance can be seen on the left. (B.Morrison)

47. The platforms taper throughout their length from 21 to 6m, to match passenger density, a very rare feature. Silver, pink, light grey and charcoal finishes were used to create a warm welcome. A class 158 DMU waits to depart on 2nd July 1996. By 2009, there were eight trains per hour and a third platform had been opened on the south side in December 2008. (T.Heavyside)

HEALD GREEN

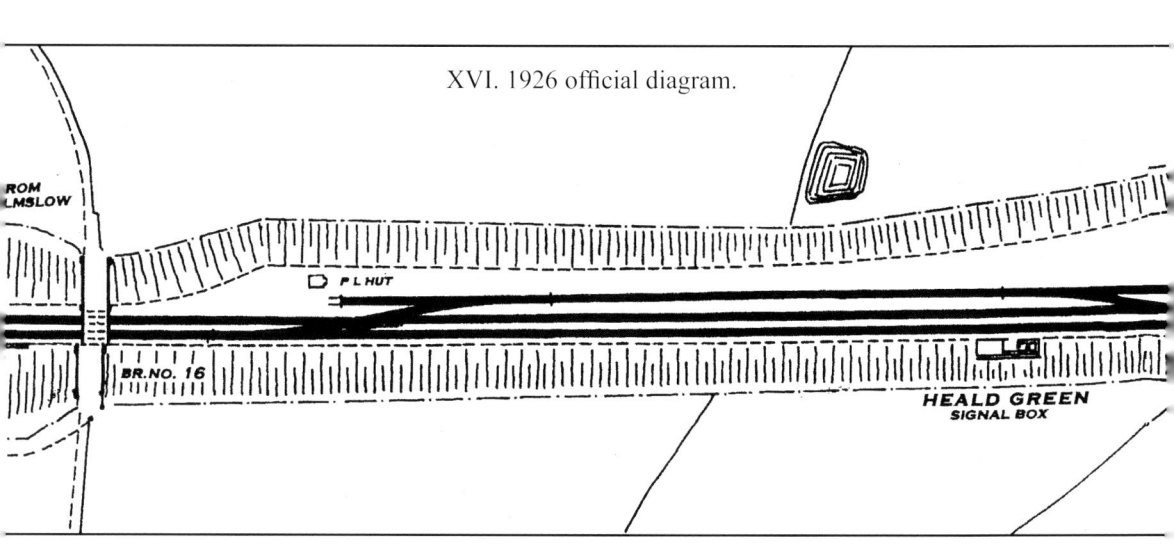

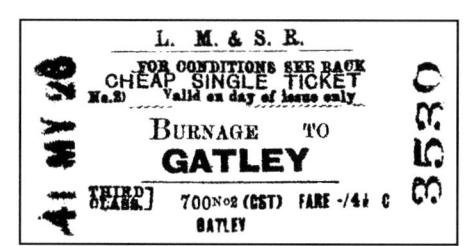

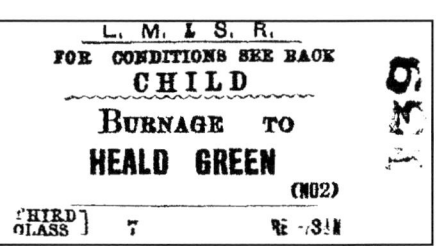

XVI. 1926 official diagram.

48. A postcard produced soon after the opening of the line includes period costume and oil lights. On the left is the entrance to the goods yard, which was in use until 25th April 1965. (P.Laming coll.)

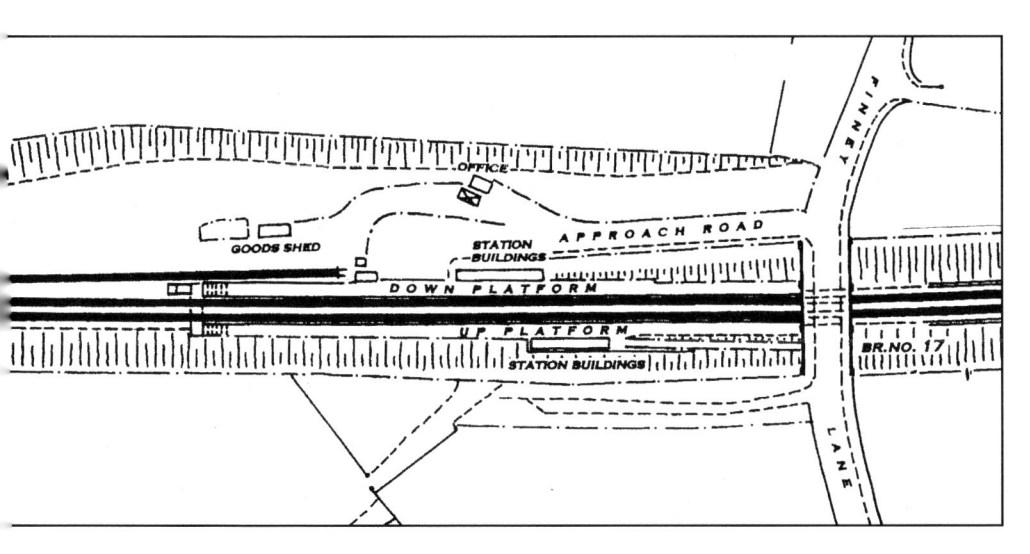

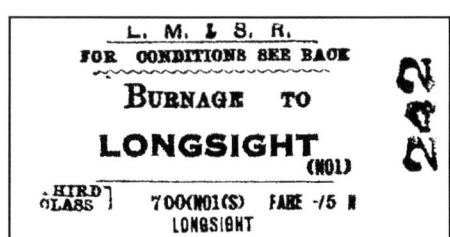

49. A motor train disgorges its passengers in the 1950s. These push-pull sets were introduced to the route in 1912. The original wooden buildings had been replaced by brick structures in 1938. They lasted for only 20 years. (Lens of Sutton coll.)

50. A 1964 record includes a southbound EMU and the new foldable push chairs, which had displaced the perambulators. The modern architecture was about five years old. (Stations UK)

51. The footbridge was added at the time of electrification and is seen on 27th April 2005. No. 158810 runs through with the 11.50 Middlesbrough - Manchester Airport TransPennine service. The bridge carries Finney Lane which marks the southern edge of the Manchester conurbation. (A.C.Hartless)

GATLEY

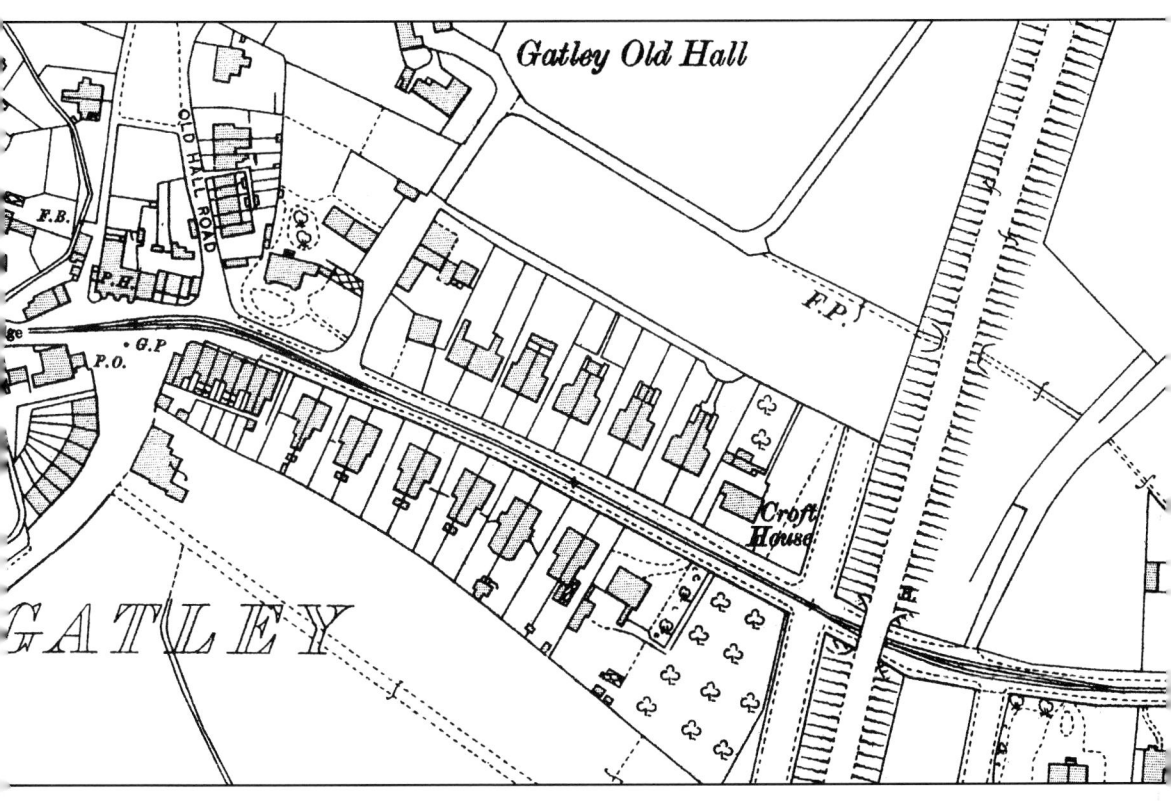

XVII. The 1909 edition shows the embankment, bridge and approach roads complete. The passing loops in the street tramway are evident.

52. The suffix "for Cheadle" was applied from 1st February 1911 until 6th May 1974. The changing of sleepers suggests that this is late in that period. (Lens of Sutton coll.)

53. An undated postcard contains a tourer of the 1920s style as a period clue. This station, plus the three to the north, were upgraded with steel platforms, access ramps, fresh lighting and new shelters in 2006-07. (Lens of Sutton coll.)

54. Worked by no. 303078, a Crewe to Manchester Piccadilly service runs in on 20th February 1988. The platform alignment has suffered, due to it being on an embankment of limited stability. (J.Whitehouse)

EAST DIDSBURY

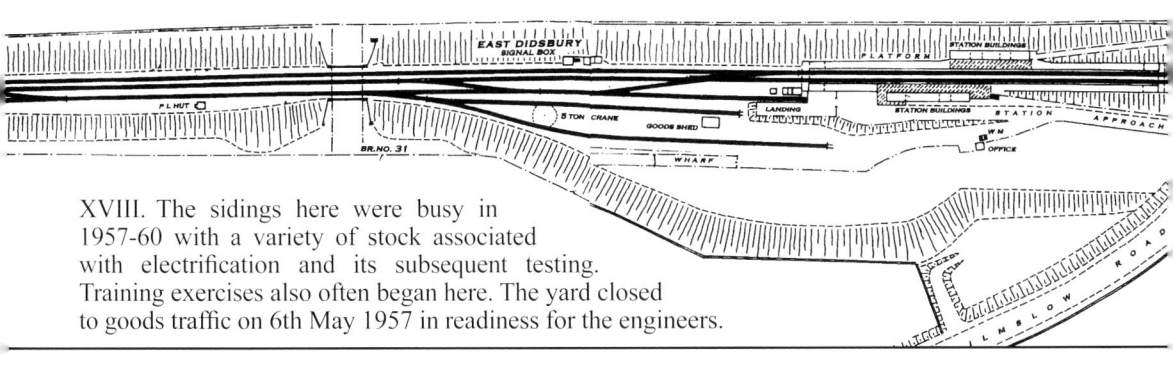

XVIII. The sidings here were busy in 1957-60 with a variety of stock associated with electrification and its subsequent testing. Training exercises also often began here. The yard closed to goods traffic on 6th May 1957 in readiness for the engineers.

55. A class 3P 2-6-2T arrives sometime in 1946. DMUs took over local services on 8th October 1956 and proved very popular. No more ash in the lap and two observation cars at no extra cost. The suffix "& Parr's Wood" was used until 6th May 1974. (Stations UK)

56. The total rebuild is evident as leaves fall on 26th October 2000. TransPennine no. 158770 passes with 09.19 Hull - Manchester Airport. The up and down side buildings are very similar, but not identical. (A.C.Hartless)

BURNAGE

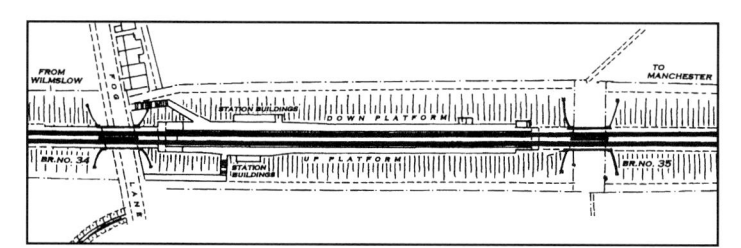

XIX. 1926 official diagram.

57. Here is the ultimate in economy: no weather protection at all. However, there was a good view from the tall embankment. Eventually urbanisation took over. There were no sidings at this station, which opened on 1st May 1910. (A.Dudman coll.)

58. Some gaze at the action on 20th April 1990, as no. 304023 arrives with the 11.42 Alderley Edge - Altrincham service. Hardly a curve to be seen in the structures. (A.C.Hartless)

MAULDETH ROAD

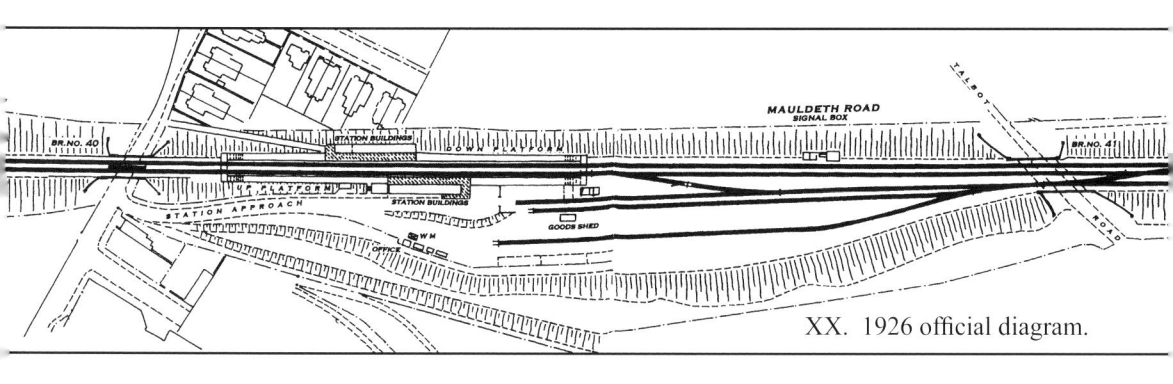

XX. 1926 official diagram.

59. The station approach road climbs up from the gates on the right to the goods yard, which closed on 5th December 1960. An inclined path served the down platform. The suffix "for Withington" was not used after 6th May 1974. (A.Dudman coll.)

60. A northward view in 1964 shows that the original building was retained on the up side only. The district became part of the City of Manchester in 1904. The route joins the main line at Slade Lane Junction, 1½ miles to the north. (Stations UK)

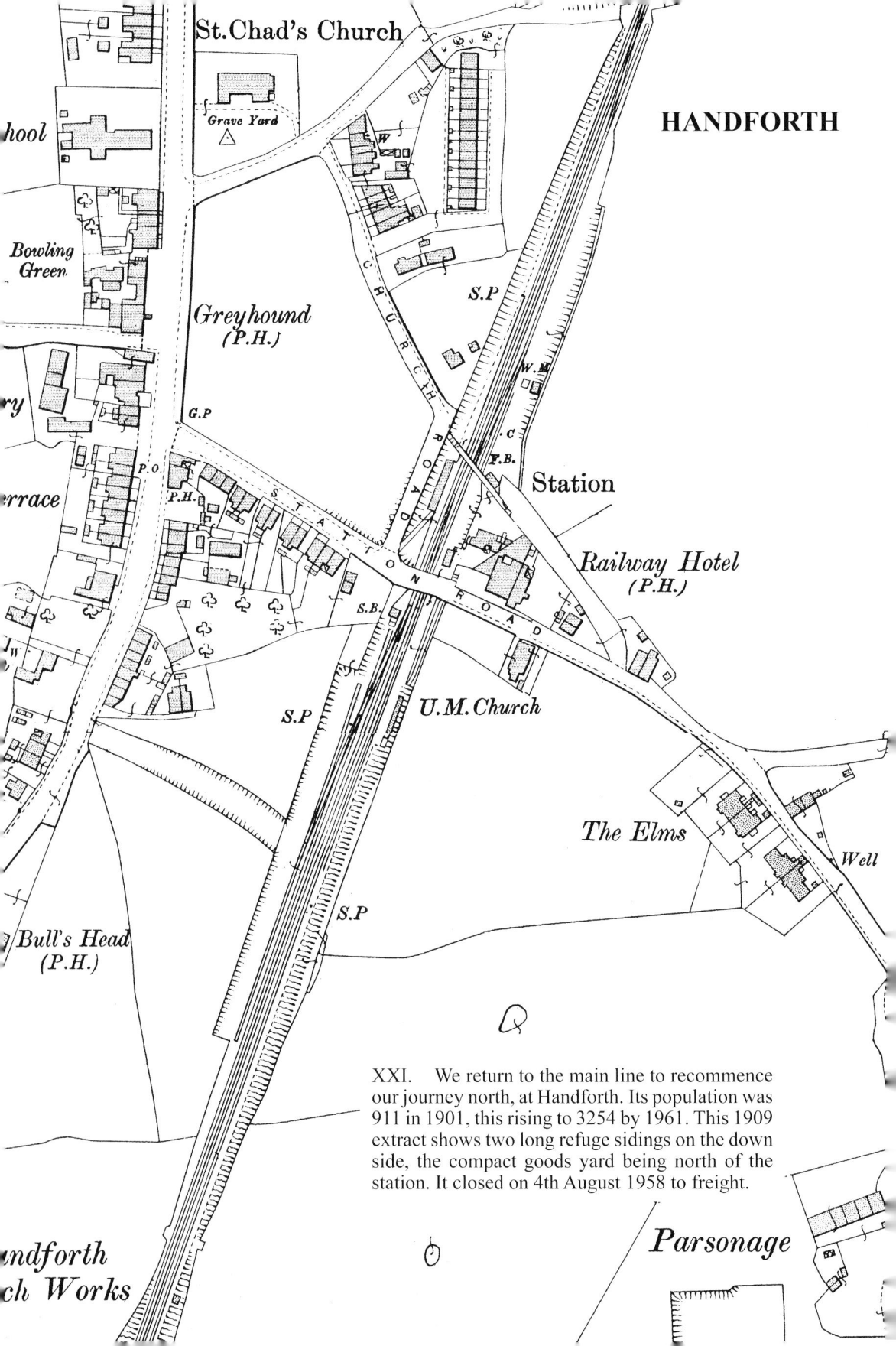

XXI. We return to the main line to recommence our journey north, at Handforth. Its population was 911 in 1901, this rising to 3254 by 1961. This 1909 extract shows two long refuge sidings on the down side, the compact goods yard being north of the station. It closed on 4th August 1958 to freight.

61. The original station had entrances on opposite sides of the track, but electrification brought new facilities at road level, with steps to the platforms. They are seen in the mid-1960s. (Lens of Sutton coll.)

62. Further rebuilding resulted in this simple entrance being provided. This is the Station Road aspect on 27th April 2005, known to some as the prospective passenger's perspective. (A.C.Hartless)

63. Seen on the same day is no. 323232 working the 15.02 Manchester Piccadilly to Crewe. The arch carries Station Road, which had earlier been the A34 trunk road. (A.C.Hartless)

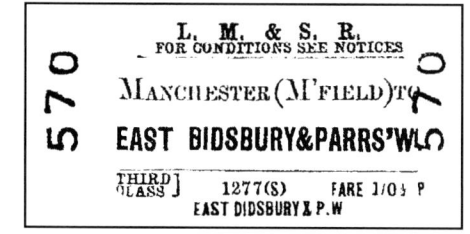

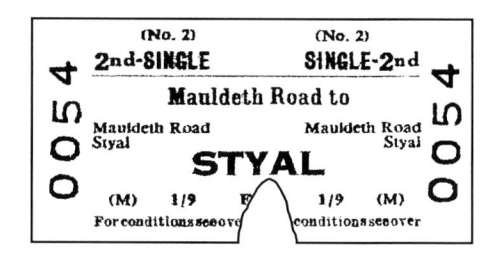

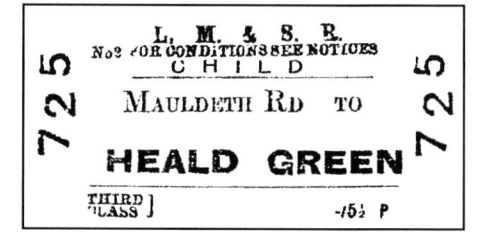

CHEADLE HULME

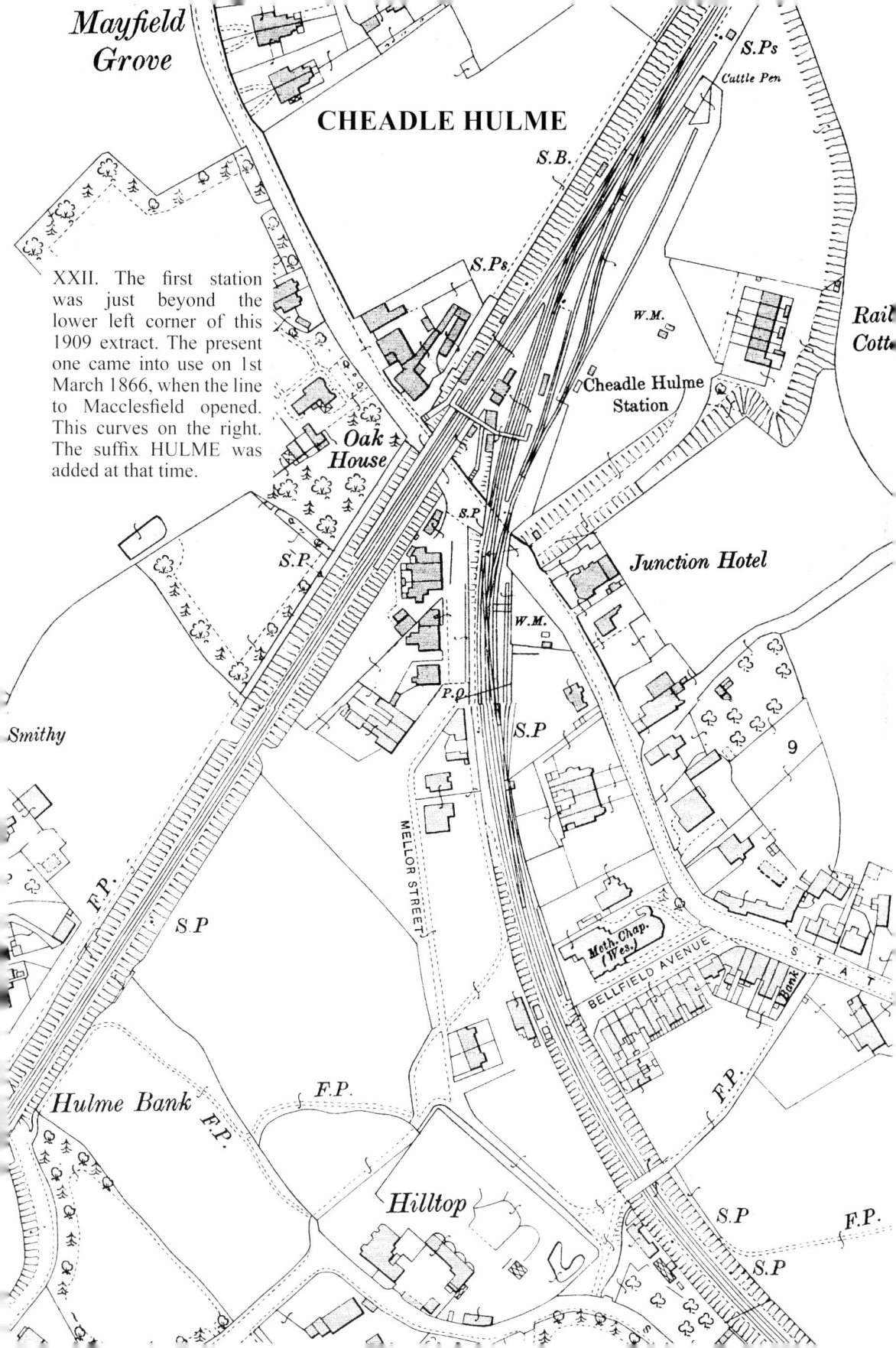

Mayfield Grove

XXII. The first station was just beyond the lower left corner of this 1909 extract. The present one came into use on 1st March 1866, when the line to Macclesfield opened. This curves on the right. The suffix HULME was added at that time.

Oak House

Cheadle Hulme Station

Cattle Pen

Rail Cott

Junction Hotel

Smithy

MELLOR STREET

Meth. Chap. (Wes.)

BELLFIELD AVENUE

Hulme Bank

Hilltop

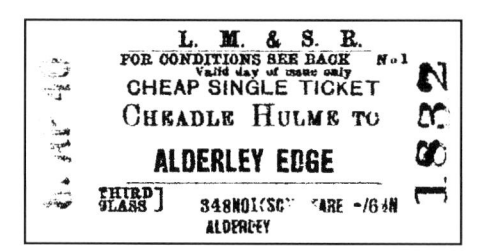

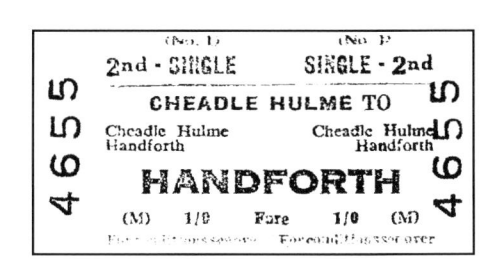

64. This unusual postcard was described as a "View from the Station". The train is departing for Wilmslow and Crewe; the curves are on the Macclesfield route. (P.Laming coll.)

65. Seen in about 1910 is another train leaving for Crewe. The population was 9044 in 1901, rising to 49,870 by 1961. The footbridge was replaced by a subway prior to electrification. (Stations UK)

66. A panorama from 1956 includes much of the goods yard, which was in use until 28th December 1964. There was another signal box further south (called No. 1) from 1899 until 1923. It contained 25 levers. (Stations UK)

67. The 17.12 Manchester Piccadilly to Euston was hauled by no. 86227 on 21st August 1976. It is seen taking the curve to Macclesfield and Stoke. This route had been electrified in 1960. (T.Heavyside)

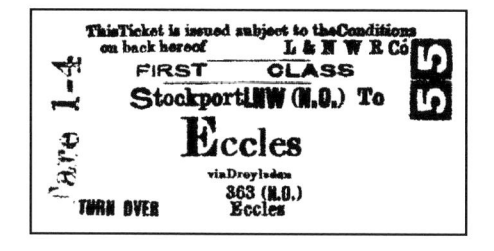

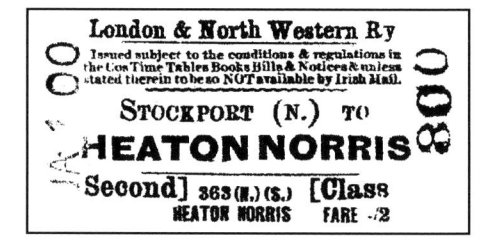

68.   Passengers stand back as a class 158 DMU speeds through on 30th October 1992, working the 10.00 Cardiff to Manchester service. The platforms seen were for 8 coaches in 2005; no. 3 took 6 and no. 4 was for 9. (A.C.Hartless)

69.   It is 30th October 1992 and no. 304013 takes the Alderley Edge line as it crosses Cheadle Hulme Junction with the 12.29 Deansgate - Crewe. Note the down starter signals for both routes, the northern end of the central platforms, the engineers siding (complete with track machine) trailing into the up Stoke line and associated ground signals. The box was built in 1901 and had 36 levers. It closed on 28th August 2000 and a panel in a Portacabin had to suffice until 1st April 2003, when Manchester South took over. Track remodelling took place in 2000. (A.C.Hartless)

SOUTH OF STOCKPORT

70. One mile south of Stockport is Adswood Road, where the quadruple track northwards commences. An up express leaves it, hauled by 4-6-0 no. 46112 *Sherwood Forester* of the "Royal Scot" class. (Bentley coll.)

71. About ½ mile south of the station is Edgeley Junction, which is seen on 21st August 1976 as no. 304012 passes while running from Altrincham to Crewe. The electrified branch runs 2½ miles to Hazel Grove, on the Hope Valley line. Overhead lines arrived in 1981. On the left is No. 1 Box, which had its 90 levers reduced to 54 in 1977. It was still in use in 2014, as was No. 2, further north. Its 54 levers control the direct line to Altrincham. (T.Heavyside)

Edgeley Shed

72.   Resting inside on 13th June 1949 is class 2F 0-6-0 no. 58377. Known as "Cauliflowers", this type was introduced by the LNWR in 1880. On the left is no. 47346, a class 3F 0-6-0T, a type produced by the LMS from 1924. (H.C.Casserley)

73.   This panorama from 25th April 1951 includes no. 58427, left of centre. It is another 2F "Cauliflower". The shed was completed in 1883 and reroofed in the 1930s. (H.C.Casserley)

74. A southward vista in June 1964 features the massive water tank, under which coaling was undertaken. The shed code was 9B from 1948 to 1968, when it closed. (T.J.Edgington/ R.S.Carpenter coll.)

75. Three photographs from April 1968 complete our survey. The ash pit is fairly clear, as coaling is in progress. No. 48745 was a class 8F 2-8-0, a type which first appeared in 1935. (T.Heavyside)

76.   Nearest is no. 44855, a class 5 4-6-0. Seriously bent rails are evident in line with the intruding diesel. (T.Heavyside)

77.   Moving onto the turntable is a class 9F 2-10-0. The shed allocation numbered 26 in 1959 and 33 in 1965. The last day for the depot was 6th May 1968. (T.Heavyside)

STOCKPORT

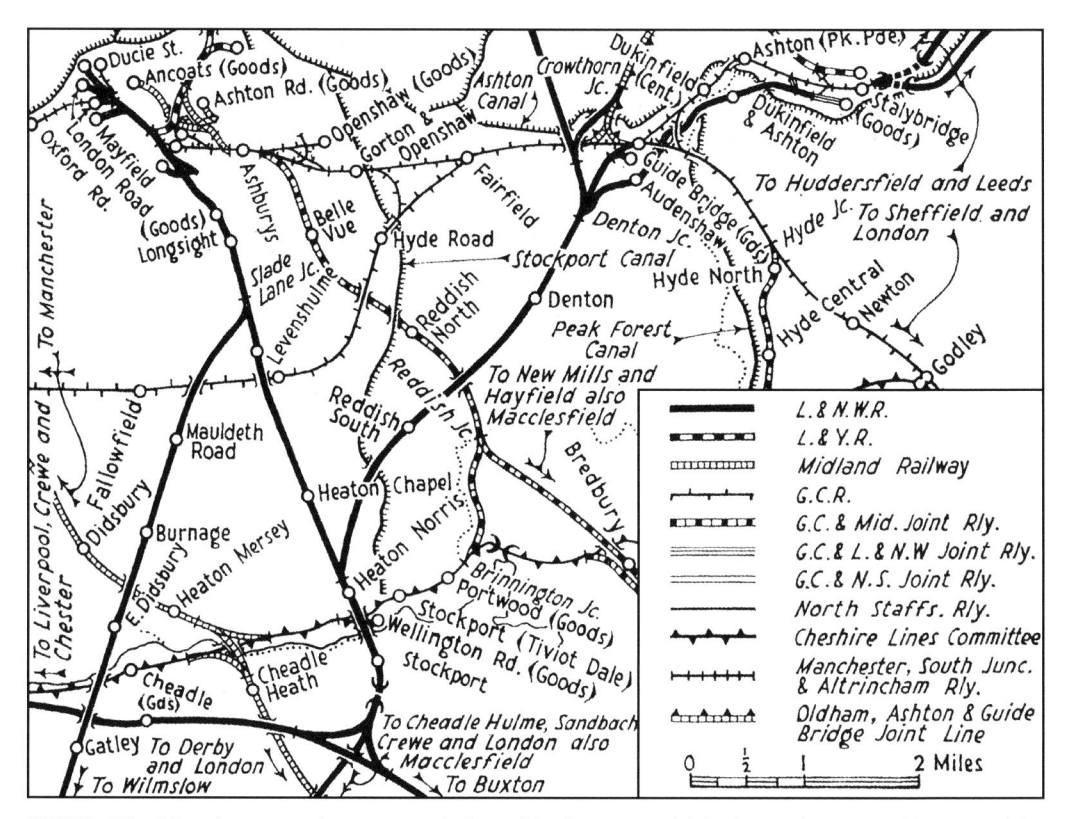

XXIII. The Manchester stations are top left on this diagram, which shows the pre-1923 ownership. The largest railways were the London & North Western, the Lancashire & Yorkshire and the Great Central. (Railway Magazine)

→ XXIV. Our journey is from bottom to top on this 1911 extract at 6ins to 1 mile. Near the centre is the main station, which carried the suffix EDGELEY from 1953 until 6th May 1968. The CLC route runs across the upper part and top right is Tiviot Dale, which was in use from 1865 to 1967. Heaton Norris is top left and its station is marked. The line lower left is to Altrincham and the one lower right is to Hazel Grove. Both carry passengers; they were reintroduced to the former route on 14th May 1989 from Altrincham and on 26th December 1991 from Chester, to aid Metrolink. Edgeley Junction No. 1, Edgeley Junction No. 2, Stockport No. 1 and Stockport No. 2 boxes were all refurbished in August 2004 as part of the West Coast Route Modernisation scheme; this included converting the last remaining mechanical points to power operation and replacing the lingering semaphore ground shunting discs with ground position colour light signals. All four signal boxes had their semaphores on the main line replaced by colour light signals for electrification of the route in 1960; the last semaphores between Crewe and Manchester were at Stockport and were abolished on 26th June 1960.

HEATON
NORRIS
Bent House Farm
Sand Pit
Hope Hill Gardens
Reservoir
Chestnut Villa
HOPE HILL
Club House Sidings
Bankfield
CHESHIRE LINES RAILWAY
George's Rd. Sidings
Church
Church Road
Recreation Ground
Stanbridge Terrace
Heaton Norris Foundry
R.C. Chap.
Tunnel
Station
Orphanage
Weir
Warren St.
Bridge St.
Market Place
Great Underbank
High Street
Chestergate
Mersey Square
St. Peter's Square
Wellington
India Mills
Heaton Lane
Travis Street
Norris Street
King Street West
River Mersey
Chestergate
HOWARD'S BUILDINGS
Parly. Boro. By.
Weirs
Brinksway Road
Sovereign Works
Recreation Ground
HOLLYWOOD PARK
Wood Street
Brook St. West
Gradwell St.
Station Road
Station
Wellington Street
Lord Street
Duke Street
John Street
Edward Street
Bamford Street
Town Hall
Union Street
Middle Hillgate
Wellington Road South
Lark Hill Road
Cunliffe Street
Freemantle Street
Farr Street
Yule Street
Aberdeen Cres.
Pitt Street
Fox Street
Greek Street
Oliver Street
Bloom Street
Adelaide Road
Carmichael Street
Chatham Street
Granville Street
Derby St.
Stopford St.
Torkington St.
Atherton St.
Castle Street
Chapel Street
James Street
Kinder Street
Shaw Heath
Workhouse
Brentnall Street
Longshut Lane West
Lyme Street
Springfield House
Heath Bank
Edgeley Road
Edgeley House
Lodge
Robinson St.
Herbert St.
Jennings St.
Hardcastle Road
Dale Street
Bowling Green
Football Ground
EDGELEY PARK
Boat Ho.
Engine Shed
Reservoirs
Edgeley Mount
Nursery
Reservoirs
Ivy House Farm
Edgeley Bleach Works
Reservoir
Village
Moscow Road
Berlin Road
Vienna Road
Petersburg Road
Stockholm Road
Dale Street South
Edgeley Junction
Engineering Works
Range Road
Menai Road
Kimberley Street
Ladysmith Street
Florist Street
Avon St.
Gilmore Street
Hat Works
Shaw Road
Adswood Road
Adswood Lane W.
Adswood Grove
Warren Road
Beech Avenue
Beech Road
CALE GREEN
L. & N.W.R.
STOCKPORT JUNCTION LINE
Bridge Hall
Stand
Cricket Ground
Bowling Greens
Club
STOCKPORT

78. A "Precursor Tank" 4-4-2T is blowing off at the up island platform in about 1910. The ridge and furrow canopies were in place from the 1890s until 1960. The gas lights lasted until 1954. There had been an average of 700 trains per day in the 1890s, 450 of which were passenger ones. (SLS coll.)

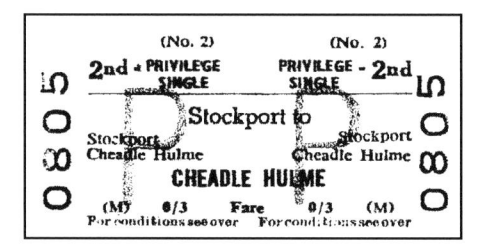

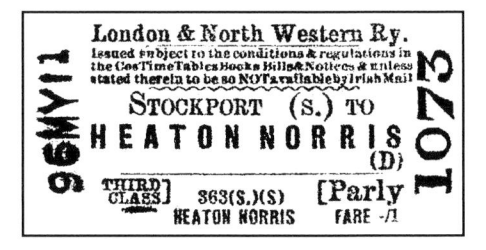

79.   A 1914 photograph features class G1 0-8-0 no. 2246 on a freight line east of the station. It is hauling a load of locomotive components packed for shipment to the Ugandan Railway. They are from the works of Naysmith Wilson in Manchester. (R.S.Carpenter coll.)

80.   It is 15th September 1944 and we see the scene obscured by the train in the previous picture. Class 4F 0-6-0 no. 4444 is passing a horse drawn cart as it approaches the massive travelling crane, capable of moving 10-ton loads. (H.C.Casserley)

81. We look north along Stockport Viaduct on 7th June 1952 when all the signalling was ex-LNWR. It has 27 spans, the highest of which is 111ft, and is 597yds in length. It was doubled in width in 1889. The gantries came down on 27th February 1955. (R.S.Carpenter coll.)

82. The map shows six tunnels south of the station. The original route had two tracks in an undivided tunnel. Gaps were made in it and three more tracks were added in 1889. Owing to limited clearances, the tops had to be removed prior to electrification and four concrete walls were built. Class G2A 0-8-0 no. 49234 is passing in May 1959, as work proceeded. (Bentley coll.)

↓ 83. No. 43190 is working the new HST service from Bristol to Manchester on 7th June 1984 and is emerging from the cutting created about 25 years earlier. The units proved to be immensely successful and two power cars gave high reliability. On the right is the 1884 No. 1 Box; its 135 levers were reduced to 98 in the 1970s. (T.Heavyside)

84. We can now enjoy three photographs from May 1988. This is from platform No. 1 and includes part of the goods yard, which had closed on 6th November 1972. No. 37258 is southbound with ballast hoppers. The subway carried a public footpath and in the 1970 improvements, a dividing fence was installed. A new frontage and ticket hall were provided at that time. (T.Heavyside)

85. Platform 1 is on the far left, while numbers 3 and 4 are on the right. The DMU is at No. 3a and is bound for Stalybridge. The number of coaches allowed at the platforms were 1-14, 2-13, 3-14, 3a-5 and 4-11. Further station improvements were undertaken in 2002-04. (T.Heavyside)

86. The Sperno rail grinding train is stabled on a former goods line. This was later lifted and a new platform was built on its site, it opening in 2006. It was numbered 0. Cardiff and King's Cross can also claim use of this unusual number. (T.Heavyside)

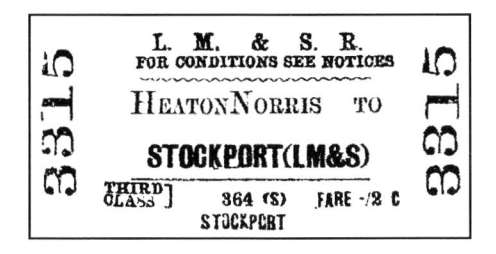

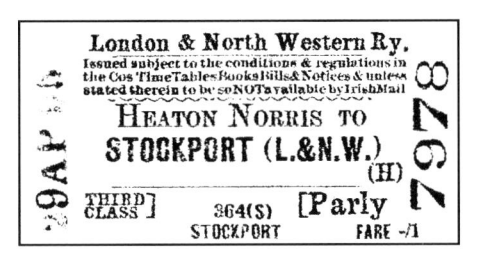

87. The 1890 No. 2 Box had its 130 lever frame cut down to 90 in the mid-1950s. No. 304016 is working from Altrincham to Alderley Edge on 4th June 1988 and is entering platform No. 1. A multitude of point rods can be seen. (T.Heavyside)

88. No. 2 Box is to be seen more fully on 7th April 2003 as no. 82115 runs in, leading the 16.27 Manchester Piccadilly to Euston services. The car is an air-conditioned driving brake van, suitable for running at 140mph. (T.Heavyside)

HEATON NORRIS

89.   Shown near the top of the last map, the station was the terminus of the line from Manchester for two years, while the Stockport Viaduct was built. It was called Stockport during this period. This is the southward view in 1947, with the lamp wires each side of the shades. The temporary station was replaced by these fine structures, which opened on 15th February 1843. (Stations UK)

90.   Looking in the other direction in the same year, we see ancient stone slabs in the foreground and historic semaphores in the background. Little changed during the 1940s, due to the war and its consequences. (Stations UK)

91. Class 4P 2-6-4T no. 42551 is working a local service to Stockport on 6th April 1954. Included is Heaton Norris No. 1 Box, which opened in 1890, its 50-lever frame being in use until 7th March 1955. (SLS coll.)

92. The station closed to passengers on 2nd March 1959 and is seen just before that event. A subway was provided to connect the four platforms. (Stations UK)

93.   The LNWR completed its massive warehouse in 1882 and it was intended for the cotton trade. An hydraulic accumulator worked the cranes and also the lifts at the station. Its tower appears at the left end of the warehouse in picture 91. The Signal & Telegraph Department workshops are on the right. Running north on an unknown date is class 5MT 2-6-0 no. 42868. (M.J.Stretton coll.)

94.   The warehouse is seen in 1964 when it was still busy. The man in the white shirt is shunting vans using a rope round a water powered capstan. The small capstans were unpowered. All Stockport area goods traffic ceased on 6th November 1972. (T.J.Edgington/R.S.Carpenter coll.)

NORTH OF HEATON NORRIS

95. Heaton Norris Junction is shown on 6th March 1958 as class 4F 0-6-0 no. 44059 comes off the Heaton Norris and Guide Bridge Line. The route was opened in 1849 and quadrupled in 1889. Beyond the smoke were the Jubilee Sidings on the approach to Reddish No. 2 Box. The flat-roofed signal box had 125 levers and had opened on 7th March 1955. Called Heaton Norris Junction, it replaced Nos 1, 2 and 3. It was still in use in 2014. (H.F.Wheeller/R.S.Carpenter coll.)

HEATON CHAPEL

XXV. The 1911 survey at 6ins to 1 mile continues from the top of the previous map. The Jubilee Sidings were completed in 1887, the year of the Golden Jubilee of Queen Victoria's reign. The station is on the left route.

96. The station opened in January 1852 and had no goods yard. An early postcard features LNWR 0-6-0 no. 1565 and the two-tone coach livery. (P.Laming coll.)

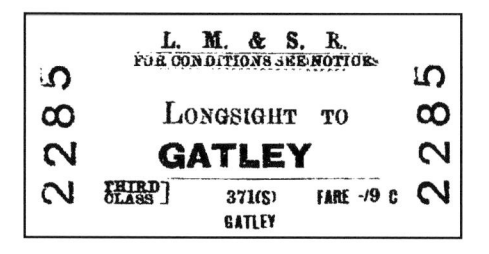

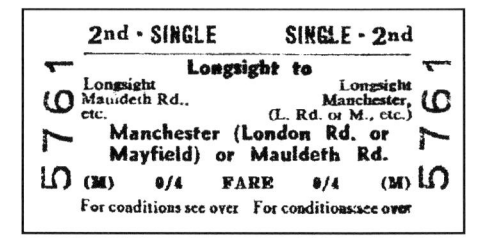

97.   Symmetry seems to have been paramount here. Polychromatic brickwork and tracery in the porch certainly added style. The suffix "& Heaton Moor" was applied from 1st January 1916 until 6th May 1974. (Lens of Sutton coll.)

98.   A 1947 southward view features a Manchester bound express at high speed. "The Pines Express" from Bournemouth West was one of the long distance workings. The 1891 signal box had two six-lever frames and was closed on 7th March 1955. (Stations UK)

99. No. 86228 *Vulcan Heritage* is northbound on 4th June 1988, while no. 304019 calls at the up platform. The class 86 locomotives were built in 1965 to 1966 and the 304 EMUs were built at Wolverton from 1960 onwards. (T.Heavyside)

100. Seen in 2005, the fine building was erected on the west side of the route at the time of the quadrupling in the 1880s. It faces Heaton Moor Road, the B5169 since 1919. (A.C.Hartless)

LEVENSHULME

101. The brick bridge lasted until 1948, when steel girders were installed. The station opened for passengers on 24th June 1842 and it replaced Rushford, which was to the north. There was a coal depot nearby until 1965. (P.Laming coll.)

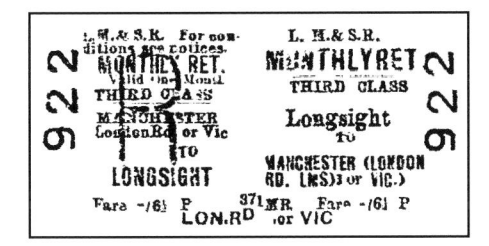

102. A 1948 panorama reveals the full extent of the canopies. From 1887 until 1910 & BURNAGE was added. The suffix NORTH was used from 15th September 1952 to the 18th June 1962. There was an 18-lever signal box here from 1884 until 17th November 1958. (Stations UK)

103. No. 86220 *Goliath* heads the "Manchester Pullman" from Euston on 17th September 1982. Tiny buildings have sufficed since about 1960 and they were still in use in 2014. Manchester University had been nearby since 1873. The train will soon reach Slade Lane Junction, where the Styal Line rejoins the main line. It is only ½ mile to the north and the 1909 Junction Box had a 40-lever frame in use until 14th December 1959. A new up platform was built in 2004 on adjustable screws to allow for fresh track ballast and/or bank settlement. (T.Heavyside)

LONGSIGHT

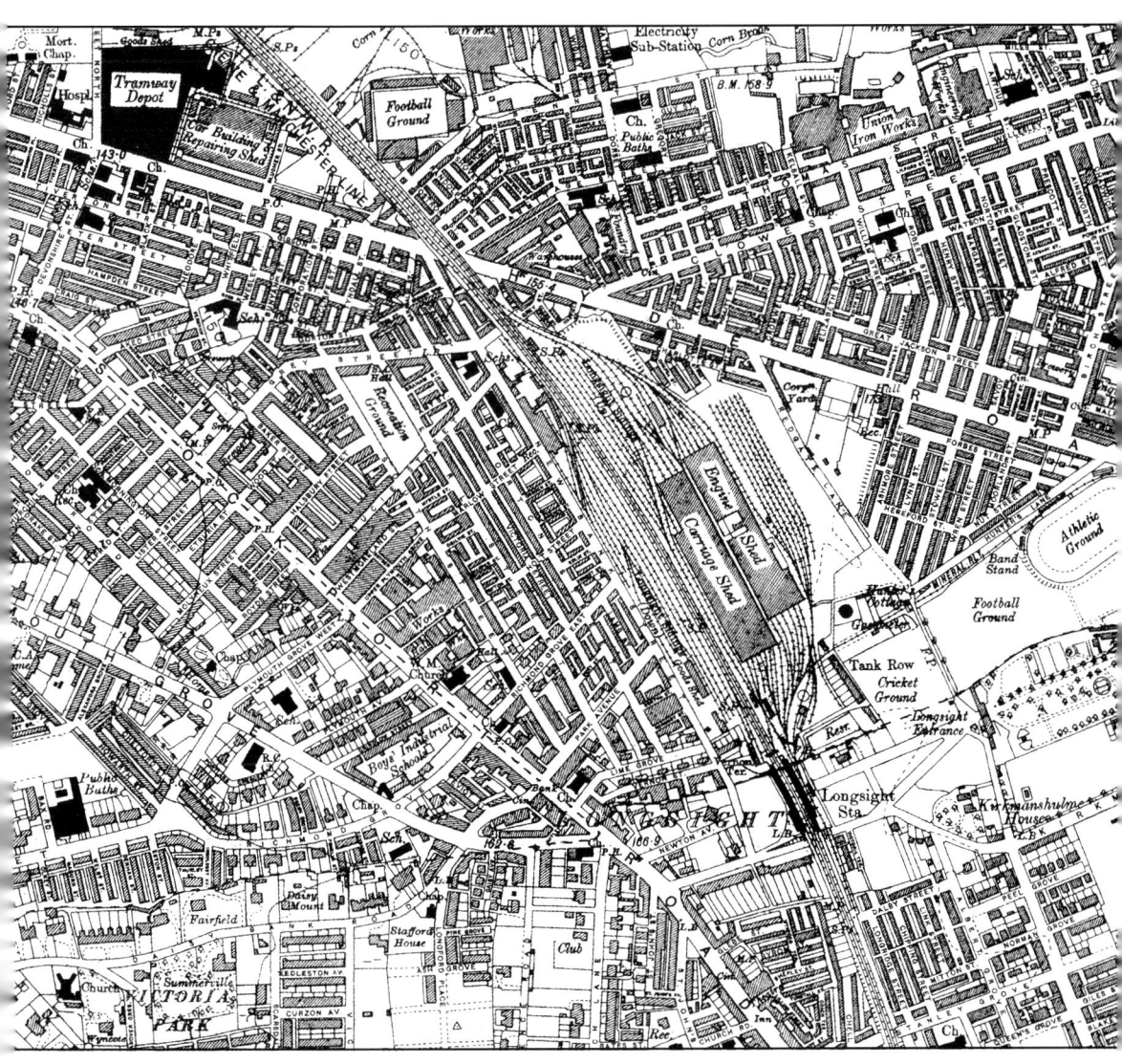

XXVI. The 1923 edition at 6ins to 1 mile includes the site of the 1842 engine shed. The station opened in April 1843 and was rebuilt for the quadrupling. The third and shorter platform was for excursions carrying visitors to the pleasure gardens and zoo called Belle Vue. This is on the right of the map, as is a "MINERAL RLY", which ran to a brewery. The parallel sidings to the right of the engine shed formed Hyde Road Coal Yard, which could take 282 wagons, while the goods yard was near New Bank Street. Their closure came on 30th January 1965. A turntable is marked: the first was 38ft, the next 50ft and the last one was 60ft long.

104. Closure to passengers came on 15th September 1958 and this 1959 view shows only the stubs of the canopy. The south end of the 1907 carriage shed is seen, with new doors fitted and soon to be known as the Electric Traction Depot. The 1934 coaling plant had been to the right of it. (A.Dudman coll.)

105. A continuation right in the same year features the engine shed, which was coded 9A. Its re-roofing had been completed in 1957. There were 128 locomotives allocated here in 1954. Closure to steam came on 14th February 1965. (R.S.Carpenter)

106. The shed for electric locomotives was built at the south end of the site and is seen on 19th July 1967. (R.S.Carpenter)

107. A short part of the old down platform was restored as a staff halt in March 1980 and was used by passengers in the Summer of 1988, during resignalling work. No. 86256 *Pebble Mill* is working the 11.00 Manchester Piccadilly to Euston Service on 13th March 1990. (T.Heavyside)

108. The South Shed of the Traction Maintenance Depot is seen on 19th March 1991. Only roads 13 to 15 are electrified and no. 17 does not enter the shed. No. 31461 stands on it and no. 47543 is on no. 18, ready for fuelling. (M.J.Stretton)

Longsight Signal Boxes

	Opened	Levers	Closed
No. 1	1903	128	1977
No. 2	1909	25	1967
No. 3	1956	35	1966
No. 4	1905	112	1959

MANCHESTER
LONDON ROAD

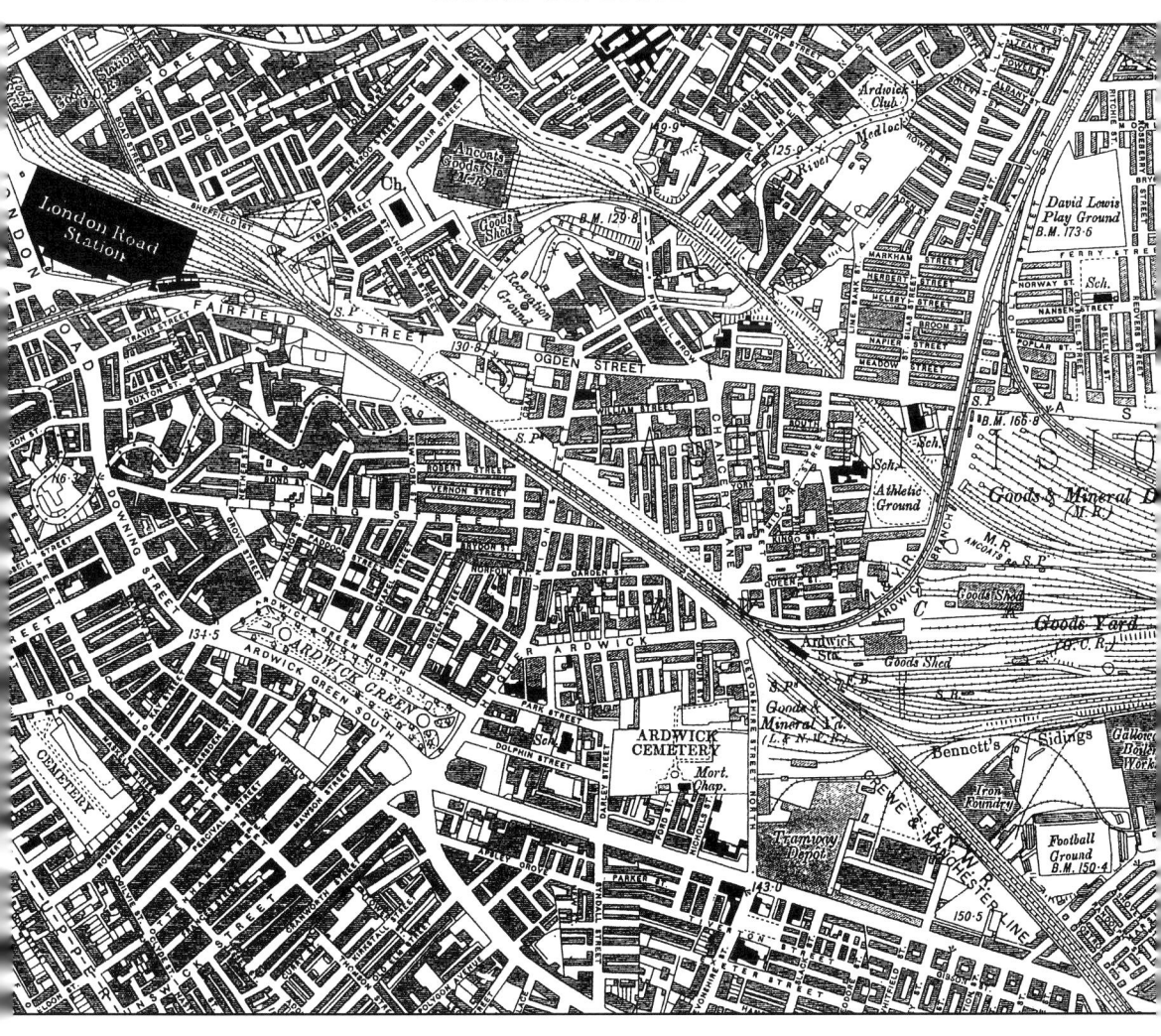

XXVII. This map overlaps the previous one and also shows the Tramway Depot. Trams first ran in the city from 1901 to 1949. Above it is Ardwick station, on the Huddersfield route. It had a down platform on the Crewe line for ticket collecting and alighting passengers from 1878 to 1902. The LNWR Ardwick Junction Box of 1907 had 112 levers and lasted until 14th December 1959. Opposite it was the GCR's No.1 Box of 1905; its 40-lever power frame worked until 1973.

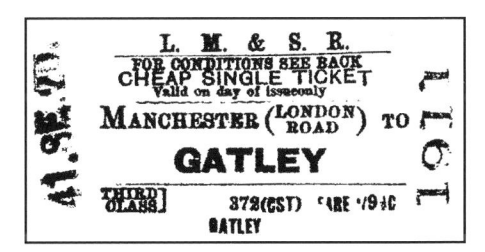

109. Seen from the west, the main building is on the right, the LNWR goods shed being on the left. Its sidings were at a low level and are top left on the map. The line on the left border is from Altrincham and enters a once separate station called Store Street, initially. Trains were electric at 1500 volts DC from 1931 to 1970 when they changed to 25kV AC. (R.M.Casserley coll.)

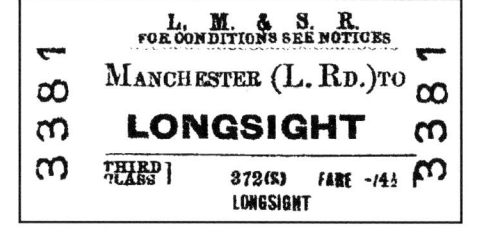

110.　Electric lighting inside the station came early in 1882, but only to the northern platforms. Running through from the west in about 1914 is "Cauliflower" class 0-6-0 no. 1010. Platforms A to C were the northern ones and 1 to 7 were behind the train, except that No. 2 did not exist. Those on the left became 12 and 13 upon renumbering. (R.S.Carpenter coll.)

111.　During the enlargement of the roof on 20th January 1866, a major failure took place, killing two workers and injuring thirty. Heavy snow was blamed. Further extension was completed in 1883. This panorama is from 1955 and we look towards the buffers. The area behind us was built on a 16-arch viaduct. No. 3 Box is included on the left. (Stations UK)

112. These are ex-LNWR starting signals and are seen at the end of platform 4 on 26th April 1955. The 1909 No. 1 Box (right) had 117 miniature levers and was fitted with a steel and concrete canopy as bomb protection in World War II. The ex-GCR box had none; it is behind the signals.
(H.F.Wheeller/
R.S.Carpenter coll.)

113. Seen on 13th June 1957 are Co-Co electric locomotives of class EM2, these working Sheffield trains via the Woodhead Tunnel. The wires carried 1500 volts DC from 1954 until 1980. Featured is No. 2 Box and beyond the left border were the four platforms of Mayfield station, which was a terminus. An extra platform was added in 1958 for use during the electrification preparations. The station was in use from 8th August 1910 until 28th August 1960.
(H.F.Wheeller/
R.S.Carpenter coll.)

MANCHESTER PICCADILLY

114. The station was controversially renamed on 12th September 1960. The Roch Valley Railway Society brought a breath of fresh steam on 28th July 1962. It is about to depart at 12.40 and the tour included the lines north of the city. Class 3P 2-6-2T no. 40063 can be seen to have 10 minutes to wait; the train returned at 7.30pm. (I.G.Holt/M.J.Stretton)

115. The splendid roof spans can be enjoyed again in 1962, after the arrival of a train of Mk.I coaches. It will be hauled out by no. E3037. The doors are open for parcels, which were diminishing in number by that time. The roadway was once packed with mailbags or newspapers. (Stations UK)

Extract from Bradshaw's Guide for 1866. (Reprinted by Middleton Press 2011)

MANCHESTER.

Telegraph stations—the Electric and International, York Street; Ducie Buildings, Exchange; 1, Mosley Street; Chapel Street, Salford; and at the Railway Stations. The Magnetic and British and Submarine, 11, Ducie Street, Exchange; 19, Bond Street; Queen's Hotel, Portland Street; 36, Thomas Street, Shudehill; Wholesale Fish Market, Great Ducie Street; Corn Exchange, Hanging Ditch (Thursdays); Lancashire and Yorkshire Railway Stations, Victoria, New Bailey Street, and Oldfield Road; Stock Exchange. The United Kingdom, Bank Street, opposite the Exchange; 1A, Cooper Street; Bonelli's, St. Ann's Square.

HOTELS.—Queen's, Thomas Johnson, first class, for families and gentlemen, recommended.

Albion, Palatine, and Clarence.

MARKET DAYS.—Tuesday (manufactures), Thursday (corn), Friday (manufactures), and Saturday (general). The Markets are Victoria, Victoria Street; Smithfield, Shudehill; Bridge Street; London Road. The Cattle Market is in Cross Lane, Salford, held on Tuesdays.

FAIRS.—Easter Monday and Tuesday, Whit-Monday, Oct. 1st, and Nov. 17th.

RACES.—In Whit-week and September.

PRINCIPAL MONEY ORDER OFFICE, Brown Street, Manchester.

BANKERS.—Cunliffes, Brooks, and Co; Heywood Brothers and Co.; James Sewell; the Consolidated, Pall Mall; Branch Bank of England; Manchester and Liverpool District Bank; Manchester and Salford Banking Co.; National Provincial Bank of England; Union Bank of Manchester; Manchester and County.

MANCHESTER, the metropolis of the cotton manufacture, a cathedral city, and parliamentary borough, in the south-east corner of Lancashire, on the Irwell, 188¼ miles from London, and 31½ from Liverpool. The last named town is the real port which supplies its staple article in the raw state, but Manchester itself has all the privileges of one, being licensed to bond imported goods as much as it it were by the sea side. It has been the head of a bishop's see since 1848, when a new diocese was taken out of Chester, including the greater part of Lancashire; and the Collegiate Church turned into a cathedral.

Manchester and Salford, though separate boroughs, divided by the Irwell, form one great town, which in 1861 contained a population of 460,428, of which 102,449 belonged to Salford.

London Road Signal Boxes

	Opened	Levers	Closed
No. 1	1908	117	25-4-1960
No. 2	1909	143	25-4-1960
No. 3	1909	26	25-4-1960
GCR	1909	84	2-1-1960
MSJ&A	1915	30	8-1-1958

116. This is London Road Power Signal Box, soon after it opened on 14th December 1959. It gradually took over the work of five nearby boxes. Travis Street passes under the rebuilt bridge, while Fairfield Street is in the foreground. A massive water tank had previously been sited here and a turntable had been beyond it. The original temporary terminus had been here. The box closed on 15th October 1988, but was not demolished until February 2008. The replacement signalling centre was located in the tower block, finished in 1960, at the front of the station. (British Railways)

117. It is 23rd February 1979 and the stage appears to have been set for four trains to rest together, while the columns display their original ornamentation. Platforms 5 and 8 are the longest, taking 17 coaches each. The electric locomotives had lost their E prefixes by that time. (J.Whitehouse)

118. No. 47147 is hauling oil tanks from the south towards Oxford Road station on 15th April 1987. It is about to pass through platform 14 and is seen from platform 9. It will soon pass over the tram terminus opened for Metrolink in 1992 - see *Triumphant Tramways* from Middleton Press. (T.Heavyside)

For other views of this station and the original route to Altrincham, see our *Chester to Manchester* album.

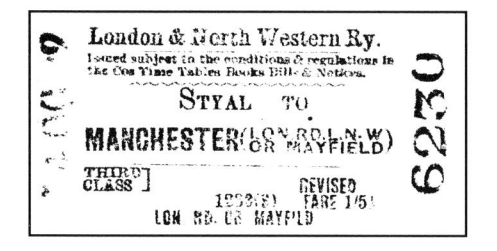

119.   Platforms 13 and 14 are the only ones to carry through trains and standing at the former on 13th March 1990 is EMU no. 303060, one of only four such units then remaining in use. It is working the 13.25 Altrincham to Crewe service. (M.J.Stretton)

120.   A photograph from the same platform on 15th August 1992 features no. 86208 *City of Chester* attached to a barrier vehicle, once used for Red Star parcels. It is working the 13.18 to Birmingham International from platform 9 and could return us to Crewe in 63 minutes, if we could put the clock back. (T.Heavyside)

Middleton Press

Easebourne Lane, Midhurst, West Sussex.
GU29 9AZ Tel:01730 813169
www.middletonpress.co.uk   email:info@middletonpress.co.uk
A-978 0 906520   B- 978 1 873793   C- 978 1 901706   D-978 1 904474
E - 978 1 906008   F - 978 1 909174

EVOLVING THE ULTIMATE RAIL ENCYCLOPEDIA

All titles listed below were in print at time of publication - please check current availability by looking at our website - www.middletonpress.co.uk or by requesting a Brochure which includes our LATEST RAILWAY TITLES also our TRAMWAY, TROLLEYBUS, MILITARY and COASTAL series

A
Abergavenny to Merthyr C 91 8
Abertillery & Ebbw Vale Lines D 84 5
Aberystwyth to Carmarthen E 90 1
Allhallows - Branch Line to A 62 8
Alton - Branch Lines to A 11 6
Andover to Southampton A 82 6
Ascot - Branch Lines around A 64 2
Ashburton - Branch Line to B 95 4
Ashford - Steam to Eurostar B 67 1
Ashford to Dover A 48 2
Austrian Narrow Gauge D 04 3
Avonmouth - BL around D 42 5
Aylesbury to Rugby D 91 3

B
Baker Street to Uxbridge D 90 6
Bala to Llandudno E 87 1
Banbury to Birmingham D 27 2
Banbury to Cheltenham E 63 5
Bangor to Holyhead F 01 7
Bangor to Portmadoc E 72 7
Barking to Southend C 80 2
Barmouth to Pwllheli E 53 6
Barry - Branch Lines around D 50 0
Bartlow - Branch Lines to F 27 7
Bath Green Park to Bristol C 36 9
Bath to Evercreech Junction A 60 4
Beamish 40 years on rails E94 9
Bedford to Wellingborough D 31 9
Birmingham to Wolverhampton E253
Bletchley to Cambridge D 94 4
Bletchley to Rugby E 07 9
Bodmin - Branch Lines around B 83 1
Bournemouth to Evercreech Jn A 46 8
Bournemouth to Weymouth A 57 4
Bradshaw's Guide 1866 F 05 5
Bradshaw's History F18 5
Bradshaw's Rail Times 1850 F 13 0
Bradshaw's Rail Times 1895 F 11 6
Branch Lines series - see town names
Brecon to Neath D 43 2
Brecon to Newport D 16 6
Brecon to Newtown E 06 2
Brighton to Eastbourne A 16 1
Brighton to Worthing A 03 1
Bristol to Taunton D 03 6
Bromley South to Rochester B 23 7
Bromsgrove to Birmingham D 87 6
Bromsgrove to Gloucester D 73 9
Broxbourne to Cambridge F16 1
Brunel - A railtour D 74 6
Bude - Branch Line to B 29 9
Burnham to Evercreech Jn B 68 0

C
Cambridge to Ely D 55 5
Canterbury - BLs around B 58 9
Cardiff to Dowlais (Cae Harris) E 47 5
Cardiff to Pontypridd E 95 6
Cardiff to Swansea E 42 0
Carlisle to Hawick E 85 7
Carmarthen to Fishguard E 66 6
Caterham & Tattenham Corner B251
Central & Southern Spain NG E 91 8
Chard and Yeovil - BLs a C 30 7
Charing Cross to Dartford A 75 8
Charing Cross to Orpington A 96 3
Cheddar - Branch Line to B 90 9
Cheltenham to Andover C 43 7
Cheltenham to Redditch D 81 4
Chester Northgate to Manchester F 51 2
Chester to Birkenhead F 21 5
Chester to Rhyl E 93 2
Chester to Warrington F 40 6
Chichester to Portsmouth A 14 7
Clacton and Walton - BLs to F 04 8
Clapham Jn to Beckenham Jn B 36 7

Cleobury Mortimer - BLs a E 18 5
Clevedon & Portishead - BLs to D180
Consett to South Shields E 57 4
Cornwall Narrow Gauge D 56 2
Corris and Vale of Rheidol E 65 9
Craven Arms to Llandeilo E 35 2
Craven Arms to Wellington E 33 8
Crawley to Littlehampton A 34 5
Crewe to Manchester F 57 4
Cromer - Branch Lines around C 26 0
Croydon to East Grinstead B 48 0
Crystal Palace & Catford Loop B 87 1
Cyprus Narrow Gauge E 13 0

D
Darjeeling Revisited F 09 3
Darlington Leamside Newcastle E 28 4
Darlington to Newcastle D 98 2
Dartford to Sittingbourne B 34 3
Denbigh - Branch Lines around F 32 1
Derwent Valley - BL to the D 06 7
Devon Narrow Gauge E 09 3
Didcot to Banbury D 02 9
Didcot to Swindon C 84 0
Didcot to Winchester C 13 0
Dorset & Somerset NG D 76 0
Douglas - Laxey - Ramsey E 75 8
Douglas to Peel C 88 8
Douglas to Port Erin C 55 0
Douglas to Ramsey D 39 5
Dover to Ramsgate A 78 9
Dublin Northwards in 1950s E 31 4
Dunstable - Branch Lines to E 27 7

E
Ealing to Slough C 42 0
Eastbourne to Hastings A 27 7
East Cornwall Mineral Railways D 22 7
East Croydon to Three Bridges A 53 6
Eastern Spain Narrow Gauge E 56 7
East Grinstead - BLs to A 07 9
East London - Branch Lines of C 44 4
East London Line B 80 0
East of Norwich - Branch Lines E 69 7
Effingham Junction - BLs a A 74 1
Ely to Norwich C 90 1
Enfield Town & Palace Gates D 32 6
Epsom to Horsham A 30 7
Eritrean Narrow Gauge E 38 3
Euston to Harrow & Wealdstone C 89 5
Exeter to Barnstaple B 15 2
Exeter to Newton Abbot C 49 9
Exeter to Tavistock B 69 5
Exmouth - Branch Lines to B 00 8

F
Fairford - Branch Line to A 52 9
Falmouth, Helston & St. Ives C 74 1
Fareham to Salisbury A 67 3
Faversham to Dover B 05 3
Felixstowe & Aldeburgh - BL to D 20 3
Fenchurch Street to Barking C 20 8
Festiniog - 50 yrs of enterprise C 83 3
Festiniog 1946-55 E 01 7
Festiniog in the Fifties B 68 8
Festiniog in the Sixties B 91 6
Ffestiniog in Colour 1955-82 F 25 3
Finsbury Park to Alexandra Pal C 02 8
Frome to Bristol B 77 0

G
Galashiels to Edinburgh F 52 9
Gloucester to Bristol D 35 7
Gloucester to Cardiff D 66 1
Gosport - Branch Lines around A 36 9
Greece Narrow Gauge D 72 2

H
Hampshire Narrow Gauge D 36 4
Harrow to Watford D 14 2

Harwich & Hadleigh - BLs to F 02 4
Hastings to Ashford A 37 6
Hawick to Galashiels F 36 9
Hawkhurst - Branch Line to A 66 6
Hayling - Branch Line to A 12 3
Hay-on-Wye - BL around D 92 0
Haywards Heath to Seaford A 28 4
Hemel Hempstead - BLs to D 88 3
Henley, Windsor & Marlow - BLa C77 2
Hereford to Newport D 54 8
Hertford & Hatfield - BLs a E 58 1
Hertford Loop E 71 0
Hexham to Carlisle D 75 3
Hexham to Hawick F 08 6
Hitchin to Peterborough D 07 4
Holborn Viaduct to Lewisham A 81 9
Horsham - Branch Lines to A 02 4
Huntingdon - Branch Line to A 93 2

I
Ilford to Shenfield C 97 0
Ilfracombe - Branch Line to B 21 3
Industrial Rlys of the South East A 09 3
Ipswich to Saxmundham C 41 3
Isle of Wight Lines - 50 yrs C 12 3
Italy Narrow Gauge F 17 8

K
Kent Narrow Gauge C 45 1
Kidderminster to Shrewsbury E 10 9
Kingsbridge - Branch Line to C 98 7
Kings Cross to Potters Bar E 62 8
Kingston & Hounslow Loops A 83 3
Kingswear - Branch Line to C 17 8

L
Lambourn - Branch Line to C 70 3
Launceston & Princetown - BLs C 19 2
Lewisham to Dartford A 92 5
Lincoln to Cleethorpes F 56 7
Lines around Wimbledon B 75 6
Liverpool Street to Chingford D 01 2
Liverpool Street to Ilford C 34 5
Llandeilo to Swansea E 46 8
London Bridge to Addiscombe B 20 6
London Bridge to East Croydon A 58 1
Longmoor - Branch Line to A 41 3
Looe - Branch Line to C 22 2
Lowestoft - BLs around E 40 6
Ludlow to Hereford E 14 7
Lydney - Branch Lines around E 26 0
Lyme Regis - Branch Line to A 45 1
Lynton - Branch Line to B 04 6

M
Machynlleth to Barmouth E 54 3
Maesteg and Tondu Lines E 06 2
Majorca & Corsica Narrow Gauge F 41 3
March - Branch Lines around B 09 1
Marylebone to Rickmansworth D 49 4
Melton Constable to Yarmouth Bch E031
Midhurst - Branch Lines of E 78 9
Midhurst - Branch Lines to F 00 0
Minehead - Branch Line to A 80 2
Mitcham Junction Lines B 01 5
Mitchell & company C 59 8
Monmouth - Branch Lines to E 20 8
Monmouthshire Eastern Valleys D 71 5
Moretonhampstead - BL to C 27 7
Moreton-in-Marsh to Worcester D 26 5
Mountain Ash to Neath D 80 7

N
Newbury to Westbury C 66 6
Newcastle to Hexham D 69 2
Newport (IOW) - Branch Lines to A 26 0
Newquay - Branch Lines to C 71 0
Newton Abbot to Plymouth C 60 4
Newtown to Aberystwyth E 41 3
North East German NG D 44 9

Northern Alpine Narrow Gauge F 37 6
Northern France Narrow Gauge C 75 8
Northern Spain Narrow Gauge E 83 3
North London Line B 94 7
North of Birmingham F 55 0
North Woolwich - BLs around C 65 9
Nottingham to Lincoln F 43 7

O
Ongar - Branch Line to E 05 5
Orpington to Tonbridge B 03 9
Oswestry - Branch Lines around E 60 4
Oswestry to Whitchurch E 81 9
Oxford to Bletchley D 57 9
Oxford to Moreton-in-Marsh D 15 9

P
Paddington to Ealing C 37 6
Paddington to Princes Risborough C819
Padstow - Branch Line to B 54 1
Pembroke and Cardigan - BLs to F 29 1
Peterborough to Kings Lynn E 32 1
Plymouth - BLs around B 98 5
Plymouth to St. Austell C 63 5
Pontypool to Mountain Ash D 65 4
Pontypridd to Merthyr F 14 7
Pontypridd to Port Talbot E 86 4
Porthmadog 1954-94 - BLa B 31 2
Portmadoc 1923-46 - BLa B 13 8
Portsmouth to Southampton A 31 4
Portugal Narrow Gauge E 67 3
Potters Bar to Cambridge D 70 8
Princes Risborough - BL to D 05 0
Princes Risborough to Banbury C 85 7

R
Reading to Basingstoke B 27 5
Reading to Didcot C 79 6
Reading to Guildford A 47 5
Redhill to Ashford A 73 4
Return to Blaenau 1970-82 C 64 2
Rhyl to Bangor F 15 4
Rhymney & New Tredegar Lines E 48 2
Rickmansworth to Aylesbury D 61 6
Romania & Bulgaria NG E 23 9
Romneyrail C 32 1
Ross-on-Wye - BLs around E 30 7
Ruabon to Barmouth E 84 0
Rugby to Birmingham E 37 6
Rugby to Loughborough F 12 3
Rugby to Stafford F 07 9
Ryde to Ventnor A 19 2

S
Salisbury to Westbury B 39 8
Sardinia and Sicily Narrow Gauge F 50 5
Saxmundham to Yarmouth C 69 7
Saxony Narrow Gauge D 47 0
Seaton & Sidmouth - BLs to A 95 6
Selsey - Branch Line to A 04 8
Sheerness - Branch Line to B 16 2
Shenfield to Ipswich E 96 3
Shrewsbury - Branch Line to A 86 4
Shrewsbury to Chester E 70 3
Shrewsbury to Crewe F 48 2
Shrewsbury to Ludlow E 71 5
Shrewsbury to Newtown E 29 1
Sierra Leone Narrow Gauge D 28 9
Sirhowy Valley Line E 12 3
Sittingbourne to Ramsgate A 90 1
Slough to Newbury C 56 7
South African Two-foot gauge E 51 2
Southampton to Bournemouth A 42 9
Southend & Southminster BLs E 76 5
Southern Alpine Narrow Gauge F 22 2
Southern France Narrow Gauge C 47 5
South London Line B 46 6
South Lynn to Norwich City F 03 1
Southwold - Branch Line to A 15 4

Spalding - Branch Lines around E
Stafford to Chester F 34 5
St Albans to Bedford D 08 1
St. Austell to Penzance C 67 3
St. Boswell to Berwick F 44 4
Steaming Through Isle of Wight A
Steaming Through West Hants A 6
Stourbridge to Wolverhampton E 1
St. Pancras to Barking D 68 5
St. Pancras to Folkestone E 88 8
St. Pancras to St. Albans C 78 9
Stratford to Cheshunt F 53 6
Stratford-u-Avon to Birmingham D
Stratford-u-Avon to Cheltenham C
Sudbury - Branch Lines to F 19 2
Surrey Narrow Gauge C 87 1
Sussex Narrow Gauge C 68 0
Swanley to Ashford B 45 9
Swansea - Branch Lines around F
Swansea to Carmarthen E 59 8
Swindon to Bristol C 96 3
Swindon to Gloucester D 46 3
Swindon to Newport D 30 2
Swiss Narrow Gauge C 94 9

T
Talyllyn 60 E 98 7
Taunton to Barnstaple B 60 2
Taunton to Exeter C 82 6
Taunton to Minehead F 39 0
Tavistock to Plymouth B 88 6
Tenterden - Branch Line to A 21 5
Three Bridges to Brighton A 35 2
Tilbury Loop C 86 4
Tiverton - BLs around C 62 8
Tivetshall to Beccles D 41 8
Tonbridge to Hastings A 44 4
Torrington - Branch Lines to B 37
Towcester - BLs around E 39 0
Tunbridge Wells BLs A 32 1

U
Upwell - Branch Line to B 64 0

V
Victoria to Bromley South A 98 7
Victoria to East Croydon A 40 6
Vivarais Revisited E 08 6

W
Walsall Routes F 45 1
Wantage - Branch Line to D 25 8
Wareham to Swanage 50 yrs D0
Waterloo to Windsor A 54 3
Waterloo to Woking A 38 3
Watford to Leighton Buzzard D 4
Welshpool to Llanfair E 49 9
Wenford Bridge to Fowey C 09 3
Westbury to Bath B 55 8
Westbury to Taunton C 76 5
West Cornwall Mineral Rlys E 04
West Croydon to Epsom B 08 4
West German Narrow Gauge D 9
West London - BLs of C 50 5
West London Line B 84 8
West Wiltshire - BLs of D 12 8
Weymouth - BLs A 65 9
Willesden Jn to Richmond B 71
Wimbledon to Beckenham C 58
Wimbledon to Epsom B 62 6
Wimborne - BLs around A 97 0
Wisbech - BLs around C 01 7
Witham & Kelvedon - BLs a E 82
Woking to Alton A 59 8
Woking to Portsmouth A 25 3
Woking to Southampton A 55 0
Wolverhampton to Shrewsbury
Worcester to Birmingham D 97
Worcester to Hereford D 38 8
Worthing to Chichester A 06 2
Wrexham to New Brighton F 47
Wroxham - BLs around F 31 4

Y
Yeovil - 50 yrs change C 38 3
Yeovil to Dorchester A 76 5
Yeovil to Exeter A 91 8
York to Scarborough F 23 9